Group Chart

Group _____   Text _____   date

Students	Skills									Comments

©The Education Center, Inc. • TEC802

Group Chart

Group _____   Text _____   date

Students	Skills									Comments

©The Education Center, Inc. • TEC802

Group Chart

Group _____   Text _____

date

Skills

Students   Comments

Group Chart

Group _____   Text _____

date

Skills

Students   Comments

Increasing Fluency with High Frequency Word Phrases

Grade 1

Developed by
Edward Fry, Ph.D. and
Timothy Rasinski, Ph.D.

on a **bus**
bowl of **cereal**
eating **fruit**

Author

Kathleen Knoblock

SHELL EDUCATION

Editor
Jenni Corcoran, M.Ed.

Assistant Editor
Leslie Huber, M.A.

Editorial Director
Dona Herweck Rice

Editor-in-Chief
Sharon Coan, M.S.Ed.

Editorial Manager
Gisela Lee, M.A.

Creative Director
Lee Aucoin

Illustration Manager
Timothy J. Bradley

Illustrators
Timothy J. Bradley
Mira Fraser

Imaging
Damco Solutions Ltd.
Sandra Riley

Consultants
Edward Fry, Ph.D.
Tim Rasinski, Ph.D.

Publisher
Corinne Burton, M.A.Ed.

Shell Education
5301 Oceanus Drive
Huntington Beach, CA 92649-1030
http://www.shelleducation.com
ISBN 978-1-4258-0288-2
© *2007 Shell Educational Publishing, Inc.*
Reprinted 2013

Table of Contents

Standards Correlations 4

About the Developers 5

How to Increase Fluency with High Frequency Word Phrases 6

How to Use This Book 7

Techniques for Engaging Students in Oral Reading 11

A Three-Component Rubric for Assessing Fluency 12

Lesson Plans 13

Answer Key. 93

References 96

The lessons marked with an asterisk (*) are special units. For more about them, see page 10.

Phrasing for Fluency Lesson	Based on Fry's Level 3 Instant Words (626–1325)	Reading with Expression (Prosody Skill Focus)	Page Number
Lesson 1	Instant Words 1–5, Noun Group 1	Naming Words	page 13
Lesson 2	Instant Words 6–10, Noun Group 2	Word Order	page 17
Lesson 3	Instant Words 11–15, Noun Group 3	Prepositions	page 21
Lesson 4	Instant Words 16–20, Noun Group 4	Phrase Chunks	page 25
Lesson 5	Instant Words 21–25, Noun Group 5	Getting the Sounds	page 29
Lesson 6	Instant Words 26–30, Noun Group 6	Stress	page 33
Lesson 7*	Instant Words 31–35, Noun Group 7	Rhyming Sounds	page 37
Lesson 8*	Instant Words 36–40, Noun Group 8	Rhythm	page 41
Lesson 9	Instant Words 41–45, Noun Group 9	Chunking for Smoothness	page 45
Lesson 10	Instant Words 46–50, Noun Group 10	Sound-Alikes	page 49
Lesson 11	Instant Words 51–55, Noun Group 11	Sentence or Phrase?	page 53
Lesson 12	Instant Words 56–60, Noun Group 12	Pitch	page 57
Lesson 13	Instant Words 61–65, Noun Group 13	Stopping for Periods	page 61
Lesson 14	Instant Words 66–70, Noun Group 14	Word Variants	page 65
Lesson 15*	Instant Words 71–75, Noun Group 15	Directions	page 69
Lesson 16	Instant Words 76–80, Noun Group 16	Sound and Sense	page 73
Lesson 17*	Instant Words 81–85, Noun Group 17	Comparing Words	page 77
Lesson 18	Instant Words 86–90, Noun Group 18	Exclamations!	page 81
Lesson 19	Instant Words 91–95, Noun Group 19	Proofreading	page 85
Lesson 20*	Instant Words 96–100, Noun Group 20	Reader's Theater	page 89

Shell Education is committed to producing educational materials that are research- and standards-based. In this effort, we have correlated all of our products to the academic standards of all 50 states, the District of Columbia, and the Department of Defense Dependent Schools. You can print a correlations report customized for your state directly from our website at **http://www.shelleducation.com**.

The No Child Left Behind legislation mandates that all states adopt academic standards that identify the skills students will learn in kindergarten through grade twelve. While many states had already adopted academic standards prior to NCLB, the legislation set requirements to ensure the standards were detailed and comprehensive.

Standards are designed to focus instruction and guide adoption of curricula. Standards are statements that describe the criteria necessary for students to meet specific academic goals. They define the knowledge, skills, and content students should acquire at each level. Standards are also used to develop standardized tests to evaluate students' academic progress.

In many states today, teachers are required to demonstrate how their lessons meet state standards. State standards are used in the development of all of our products, so educators can be assured they meet the academic requirements of each state.

To print a correlations report for this product, visit our website at **http://www.shelleducation.com** and follow the on-screen directions. If you require assistance in printing correlations reports, please contact Customer Service at (877) 777-3450.

McREL Compendium

Shell Education uses the Mid-continent Research for Education and Learning (McREL) Compendium to create standards correlations. Each year, McREL analyzes state standards and revises the compendium. By following this procedure, they are able to produce a general compilation of national standards.

The reading comprehension strategies assessed in this book are based on the following McREL content standards. All of the following standards apply to each lesson in this book.

1. The student understands level-appropriate sight words and vocabulary (e.g., words for persons, places, things, actions; high-frequency words).

2. The student reads aloud familiar stories, poems, and passages with fluency and expression (e.g., rhythm, flow, meter, tempo, pitch, tone, intonation).

3. The student uses mental images based on pictures and print to aid in comprehension of text.

4. The student uses basic elements of phonetic analysis (e.g., common letter/ sound relationships, beginning and ending consonants, vowel sounds, blends, word patterns) to decode unknown words.

5. The student uses basic elements of structural analysis (e.g., syllables, basic prefixes, suffixes, root words, compound words, spelling patterns, contractions) to decode unknown words.

About the Developers

Dr. Timothy Rasinski is a well-established authority in the fluency area of reading instruction. His many speaking appearances to teachers, as well as his landmark book, *The Fluent Reader* (Scholastic 2003), have introduced the concept of fluency to thousands of teachers.

Dr. Edward Fry has a decade-long association with a research-based, high-frequency list of words known as the *Instant Words*. He is also a frequent conference speaker, and his most widely used book is *The Reading Teacher's Book of Lists* (Jossey Bass, 5th Edition 2006).

Key themes of this grade-level book for classroom teachers come from elements of these two books: "chunking," or reading phrases as units, from Dr. Rasinski, and the rank ordering of the *Instant Words* from Dr. Fry.

Chunking is seen in the introductory phrases of each lesson, where each phrase contains a grade-leveled Instant Word. Each of the phrases is also incorporated into a sample story in order to add meaning and improve fluency (Rasinski and Padak 1998).

The ordering of the Instant Words is important because it helps to answer the question, "Which words should I teach first, then next, etc.?" The answer comes from computer-based research that counts the frequency of millions of words in books, curriculum materials, and magazines (Carroll 1971, Sakiey 1977, Fry 2000).

Both Dr. Rasinski and Dr. Fry are indebted to Dr. Jay Samuels at the University of Minnesota, who is a real pioneer in the field of fluency. His article in the 1979 *Reading Teacher* entitled "The Method of Repeated Reading" is regarded as a classic. Dr. Samuels has additional published research on the subject of fluency that has been a beneficial resource to those in the field (Samuels 2002).

The authors of this Shell Education series strongly agree that improving reading comprehension is important and that improved fluency contributes to improved comprehension. To further stress comprehension, each lesson contains a set of questions about elements such as main idea, details, vocabulary, and subjective or creative interpretations.

The authors further agree that this is not a "speed reading" course. While reading rate is an important aspect of fluency, so are the many elements of expression and prosody. Experienced teachers can tell a lot about a student's comprehension of a written passage by simply listening to him or her read aloud.

Professor Rasinski also has an interest in the use of reader's theater and poetry for repeated readings and, therefore, fluency development. Hence, in this book you will find the use of dialogue within the stories, as well as the use of poetry—all intended to enhance students' fluency development and enjoyment of learning.

Professor Fry is interested in the elements that make up prosody, such as pitch (high or low voice), punctuation, stress, pauses, and many others. These elements are partly based on *The Cambridge Encyclopedia of the English Language* by David Crystal.

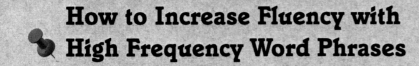

How to Increase Fluency with High Frequency Word Phrases

Components and General Guidelines

On the road to becoming readers, students must not only learn to read and recognize words, but also recognize how combinations of words affect meaning. Although essential, word recognition and comprehension are not what make a reader fluent. To become fluent, students must also be able to read at a smooth pace and with appropriate expression. Can expression be taught? Yes! Students can be taught to use structural and contextual evidence in writing as clues for how to read. Students can also be taught strategies for recognizing mood, purpose, emotion, and other interpretive skills that they can then use to enhance expression. The lessons in this book target the three major components of fluency: accuracy, rate of reading, and expression.

However, no matter what or how much one tries to teach skills to students, one more critical component must be provided with regularity—the opportunity to hear fluent reading! This simple fact—that one must hear language in order to become fluent in it—is frequently overlooked in the classroom. That is why this product not only provides activities in which students read, write, discuss, evaluate, and study written text, but also requires students to listen to text being read fluently. A CD is included with this book that has the target phrases and the stories (or other text from each lesson) being read aloud with model fluency. Students can listen as often as necessary to both learn the words and phrases and also associate the written words and sentences in the passage with how they should sound.

The authors highly recommend that teachers frequently have students listen to model reading, and also that each list of phrases and reading selections be read and reread aloud several times. Students need ample exposure to model oral language and many opportunities to practice reading aloud themselves.

Materials Included in This Product

- 20 four-page lessons include Fry Word Phrases, stories or other text selections, writing, comprehension, learning and applying prosody, fluency checkpoint, and a student evaluation
- Fluency Assessment Rubric and a reference list of oral reading fluency strategies
- Audio CD includes oral readings of the phrase lists and reading selections in each lesson
- Data CD includes copies of each reading selection for printing or making transparencies

Suggested Additional Materials

- A notebook or folder for each child to keep lesson materials and writing paper

The Lessons—A Comprehensive Approach

This book combines two research-based approaches to teaching reading: **instant words** and **phrasing**. Together, they are powerful tools for building fluency. Many teachers of reading are familiar with Fry's Instant Words. These words are listed in order of their frequency encountered in typical written material. The first 25 words make up about one-third of all printed material; the first 100, about half. Words 1–3000 have been roughly divided into six leveled lists in Dr. Fry's *Spelling Book*. Below is the breakdown by level:

Level 1: Instant Words 1–100	Level 4: Instant Words 1326–2025
Level 2: Instant Words 101–625	Level 5: Instant Words 2026–2725
Level 3: Instant Words 626–1325	Level 6: Instant Words 2726–3000

Dr. Fry's Spelling Book Levels 1–6: Words Most Needed Plus Phonics by Edward Fry, Ph.D.
© 1999, Teacher Created Materials, Inc.

The lessons in this book are based on Fry's *Instant Words*. At this level, Fry's First 100 *Instant Words* are introduced sequentially, divided into 20 lessons. The words in each lesson are used in the story in which they are introduced. Whenever possible, words from previous lessons are used in the stories. The lessons, therefore, should be done in order.

Especially for Level 1

Two format elements are included at this level to make the lessons easy to follow. All text intended to be read aloud by the teacher appears in italics. The directions for students are simplified and accompanied by simple icons that help them make sure they know what to do.

Instant Words

The instant words are presented first in isolation. Students follow along as they listen to the words read to them. They then practice listening to and reading the words themselves.

Phrases

The instant words in the lesson are introduced in phrases that will appear in the story. These phrases are intended to be read aloud to students and practiced before continuing on.

Story

Each lesson has a story or other text for students to practice and read. The phrases appear in bold print in the story. They should be reread often. They can also be listened to on the audio CD.

About the Story (Comprehension and Test Preparation)

Here the student moves from literal reading of phrases and sentences to understanding what was read. The questions highlight vocabulary, general understanding, and simple analysis. In the latter part of the book, the questions may require higher-level thinking and open-ended responses.

On Your Own

In this section, students are asked to work with words, phrases, or concepts from the story. They may also be asked to make connections, apply a concept, or identify relationships between certain types of words.

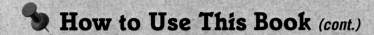

How to Use This Book *(cont.)*

Learning About Reading (Prosody Skill)

Each lesson focuses on a specific skill related to learning about reading as a function of total language fluency. Rather than targeting such things as rules and word-attack skills, this section takes more of an analysis- and strategy-approach to interpreting the written language. By learning about reading, along with learning to read, students are taking steps to becoming fluent readers—reading with accuracy, at a good rate, smoothly, and with meaningful expression. Although written "to the student," the lesson is intended to be read aloud by the teacher.

Try It!

Here students have the opportunity to try the skill they've just learned. They have to apply it in some way either by using the story they read in the lesson or with new text.

Fluency Checkpoint

Within each lesson is a fluency checkpoint, which suggests that students reread the passage until they not only get all the words right, but also read it smoothly and with meaning (expression). The teacher can suggest that they practice as if they were rehearsing it for a performance—repeating as many times as needed to be able to read it fluently.

Evaluation

Each lesson concludes with a student evaluation. Sometimes students will evaluate their own reading and feelings toward it; other times they are asked to work with a partner or group. The purpose is to encourage student reflection and ownership for one's own learning.

A Word About Reading Rate

Although the greater part of the lessons are devoted to accuracy, comprehension, and expression in oral reading, the rate of reading, or pace, is also a component of fluency. As students become more adept at reading through the other aspects of fluency, their rate of reading should continue to improve. Intermittently, but at least three times a year, do a formal fluency reading rate to check on each student. Make sure to use a passage with which the student has had opportunities to practice and rehearse both the text and reading with proper expression. Then, have him or her read it aloud for exactly one minute. Record the number of words the student read accurately in one minute. Use this guide in determining general expectations for reading average, grade-level materials.

	NUMBER OF WORDS READ CORRECTLY IN ONE MINUTE		
Grade Level	First 1/3 of year	Middle of year	Last 1/3 of year
1		30	60
2	50	80	95
3	80	95	110
4	100	110	120
5	105	120	130
6	115	130	145

**Adapted from *The Fluent Reader*
by Timothy Rasinski, © 2003 Scholastic**

Pacing

With 20 lessons and about 36 weeks of school in a typical year, teachers do not need to feel rushed to complete a certain number of activities every week. Teachers can spread out the lessons by tailoring them to individual preferences and student needs. Keep in mind, though, that the lessons introduce words and phrases in sequential order, so it would best serve the students to teach them in this order.

Spend a little time each day, for at least a week, on pacing within a single lesson. The pacing plan that follows is just one suggestion.

Monday	· Distribute copies of the first page of the lesson. Read and reread the list of phrases. Talk about them. Do additional activities as needed. · Model reading the story with expression. Discuss it briefly and read it again. Allow students to practice reading the phrases and story as much as necessary. · Make the CD readings available so students can listen to the readings of the phrases and the story. Keep this listening station open all week and encourage students to use it any time they have a few free moments.
Tuesday	· Distribute copies of the second page of the lesson. Discuss the story read the previous day. Read or have a student read the story aloud again. Read the directions for "About the Story." Have students whisper-read the phrases and story again before completing the activity. · Distribute copies of the third page of the lesson. Read the directions for "On Your Own." If necessary, discuss further; otherwise, encourage students to do the activity independently. · As students work, take the opportunity to help anyone who needs extra support or assemble a small group for extra practice reading the words, phrases, and story.
Wednesday	· Teach the lesson at the bottom of the third page by reading the explanation aloud to students and discussing the content. Give extra examples as needed. If applicable, ask students for additional examples in the story, their reading books, or other text to check their understanding of the skill. · If desired, put examples from the lesson on the board or on chart paper to review and reteach as needed before continuing. · Distribute copies of the fourth page of the lesson. Direct students' attention to the "Try It!" section. Read the directions and clarify as needed. Allow students time to complete the activity.
Thursday	· Give students time to reread and rehearse the passage as needed—alone, in pairs, in groups, or with a classroom helper. This is an excellent time to do formal and informal fluency checks. Listen to students read, or have them read to aides, parent helpers, or even competent older students. If a teacher has no assistance, he or she can randomly choose several students to listen to each week. This way, all students will be prepared, but the teacher only needs to check a few at a time. · While checking fluency or working with individual students, have the rest of the students complete the evaluation section of the lesson.
Friday	· Use this day to continue checking fluency and/or for reteaching and review. · Teachers may want to give students a follow-up assignment relating to the story or the skill.

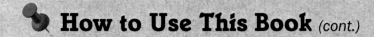

What About Differentiation?

Teachers can always extend or adapt lessons to meet their students' needs. Below are a few ideas for addressing different needs.

ELL (English Language Learners) and Others Who Need Extra Help with Language

Use the CD that accompanies this book to give students experiences with auditory-visual association, allowing them to make connections between the model reading on the CD and the text on the page. Have students use highlighters to mark certain things in the book, such as key words in the phrases, punctuation, stress, and figures of speech. To extend practice, make flash cards of the given phrases and then add other phrases, using the target instant words. For comprehension practice, try a game of "Catch Me If You Can." In this game, the teacher purposely misuses a word and the students try to "catch" the teacher's error. When reading the story or answering questions, pair students with a helper to give them the extra attention that may make the difference between trying again or giving up. When discussing stories, elicit from students ways that they can connect them to their real lives. Additional modifications include echo reading, having students create pictures (or other visual representations) of the phrases, and having students act out phrases. Be patient, and encourage students to express their feelings and ask for help.

For Those Who Always Finish First and Those Who Get Bored Easily or Can Read Well Above the Norm

First, children who excel in reading do not need to do the regular activity *plus* more. These students know busy work when they see it. Rather than give them additional work, a better approach is to give them alternate, challenging assignments from the start. For example, after reading the story, instead of the regular "On Your Own" activity, have these students do some more research on the topic, create a crossword puzzle from the instant words, write a different ending to the story, or write a different story in the same format using the same phrases from the list. These are just a few suggestions for differentiating the "On Your Own" activity, but each activity can be modified in a similar way. Choose activities that have a purpose. In other words, require the students to report on their findings, use their crossword at a center, or read their original stories to the class.

A Note About Level 1

The selected reading passages vary in a number of ways. Most are fiction, some are not. Some are longer and easier to read; others are shorter but more challenging. Throughout the lessons, the text reflects different writing genres. Note that Lessons 7, 8, 15, 17, and 20 are flagged as special. Lesson 7 introduces students to group-divided choral reading. Lesson 8 combines poetry with shared reading. Lesson 15 is all about reading and following directions. In Lesson 17, students read a letter from summer camp. Finally, Lesson 20 gives students the opportunity to participate in simple reader's theater. By exposing young students to these types of motivating reading experiences alongside the task of learning to read itself, they will already be on the road to becoming lifelong fluent readers, writers, listeners, and speakers.

Oral reading fosters fluency. Students need to hear model language in order to acquire it. Listening to good oral reading and participating in repeated reading strengthens accuracy, reading rate, and expression—the fundamentals of fluency. Here are a few ways to engage students in oral reading.

Oral Preview

Oral preview involves having students hear how the text should sound when it is read fluently before they attempt to read it themselves. This strategy is especially helpful for students who are English Language Learners or those who simply need more support. It is used in conjunction with other strategies and is the basis of every lesson in this book.

Repeated Reading

Repeated reading gives students a chance to "get to know" the text before being asked to read it aloud. The opportunity to practice increases both willingness and proficiency with regard to oral reading. This technique is highly recommended for students as they do the lessons in this book.

Paired Reading

This strategy involves two readers sharing the presentation of the text. Paired reading can include two students, a student and an adult, a student and an older student, or a student and a teacher. In its best form, paired reading involves a more proficient reader paired with a less proficient one, so that the stronger one can support the other.

Call and Response/Refrain

Call and response is a type of choral reading. One student reads a portion of a text and then the class or a small group responds by reading the next portion in unison. When the response portion is a repetition of the same text, it is called a refrain.

Divided Reading

In this version of choral reading, assigned sections of the text are read by groups of students.

Reader's Theater

In reader's theater the text is read like a script. It is like a play but with some important differences. Although the students practice for the "performance," they read, rather than memorize, their lines. Students may use simple props, but there are no costumes, sets, or "action." The script may have a few parts, many parts, and even parts that are read by all participants.

A Three-Component Rubric for Assessing Fluency

Assessing Fluency

One might think that assessing fluency only produces vague, subjective descriptions, such as "he reads well," "she reads with no expression," and so on. The goal is for students to become fluent, but fluency is not measurable by objective standards. Although fluency can't be measured with a right or wrong score, it can be assessed more accurately by using the rubric below.

Score	Accuracy	Rate (Pace)	Expression	
			Structural paraphrasing, pausing, smoothness, pitch, volume	**Interpretive** mood, purpose, emotion, subtleties of meaning
4	Recognizes most words and reads them correctly without hesitation.	Consistently reads at natural, conversational pace or as appropriate for the text.	Reads smoothly. Consistently uses meaningful phrasing and appropriate pausing. Adjusts pitch and volume to the circumstances (type of text or audience).	Recognizes different purposes for reading. Consistently conveys the appropriate mood and emotion. Distinguishes word meanings in context.
3	Recognizes pre-taught and familiar words and reads them correctly. May hesitate, but can use context and apply word-attack skills.	Sometimes reads at a conversational pace but is inconsistent. May speed up and slow down or generally read at a slightly slower pace.	Reads smoothly in general but with some breaks or misuse of pausing. Is aware of pitch and volume.	Reads most text with appropriate emphasis for the purpose and mood of the text. May at times slip into concentrating on pronunciation, but will usually recover and resume once past the problematic area.
2	Recognizes and reads some words correctly, but hesitates. Has some difficulty using context clues and applying word-attack skills.	Reads somewhat slower than appropriate for text. May have stops and starts or have to go back and reread.	Reads unevenly. May miss punctuation clues resulting in choppiness or run-on reading. Does not generally attend to pitch and volume.	May use natural-sounding language at times, but in general, frequently resorts to focus on word-by-word pronunciation without regard for the mood, purpose, or intended meaning.
1	Misreads words frequently. May not recognize words in different contexts. Is not adept at applying word-attack skills.	Reading is slow and laborious. Frequently hesitates, stops, or goes back to "start over."	Does not usually read in meaningful units, such as phrases or clauses. May read word-for-word with little attention to context or punctuation signals.	Reading is generally monotone and lacks an awareness of mood, purpose, or emotion. May not recognize word meanings in context.

Throughout this book, fluency is described as the ability to read with accuracy, with expression, and at a good rate. Note in the chart above that expression has been subdivided. For the purposes of evaluation and scoring, it may be useful to rate expression based on structural factors and interpretation separately. To record a single expression score, combine the two subcategory scores. Possible scores range from **4** (lowest) to **16** (highest). Generally, a total score of **8** or above suggests that a student is progressing in fluency. A score below **8** may indicate that fluency is a concern.

Name _____ Date _____

Instant Words

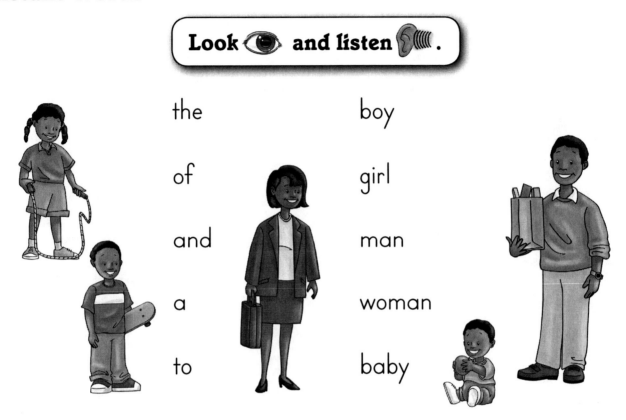

Look 👁 and listen 👂.

the	boy
of	girl
and	man
a	woman
to	baby

Phrases

Read these phrases to yourself as you listen to them being read aloud.

Look 👁, listen 👂, and read 📖.

a man	a baby	the girl
a woman	to the man and woman	the baby
a little girl	of the boy and girl	of the girl
the man	the woman	

Could you read every word? If not, repeat reading and listening until you can. Then, try reading the phrases on your own without listening.

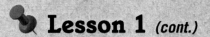

Lesson 1 (cont.)

Name _____ Date _____

Story *Read the story to yourself as you listen to it read aloud. Repeat reading and listening until you know every word.*

> **Look 👁 , listen 👂, and read 📖 .**

A man and a woman had a little girl.

Then, a baby came to the man and woman.

The baby is a boy.

This is the man, the woman, the girl, and the baby.

The man is the father of the boy and the girl.

The woman is the mother of the boy and the girl.

The baby is the brother of the girl.

About the Story *Finish each sentence with a group of words from the story.*

> **Look 👁 , listen 👂, and write ✏ .**

1. A man and a woman had _____ _____ .

2. The baby is _____ .

3. The man is the father _____ _____ and the girl.

4. The baby is the brother _____ _____ .

#50288—*Increasing Fluency with High Frequency Word Phrases Grade 1*   © *Shell Education*

Name _____ Date _____

On Your Own

Read 📖 and draw ✏️ .

a boy and a girl	a man, a girl, and a boy
the man and the woman	a woman and a baby

Learning About Reading: *Naming Words*

Listen 👂 .

You are learning to read words—by themselves and in groups. Did you know that words have jobs? Some words name things, such as people and places. Some words show actions, such as play, read, go, and come. Other words have different jobs. Knowing the jobs a word has makes learning to read easier.

Look at the list of words at the top of page 13. Can you tell which ones have the job of naming something? One way to tell if a word has the job of naming something is to ask if you can picture it in your mind. Close your eyes. Can you picture the word to? No. The word to is not a naming word. Can you picture a boy? Yes. Boy is naming word. Let's find other naming words on the list.

Name _____ Date _____

Try It! *Read each group of words. Draw a line under each naming word you find.*

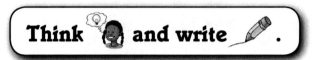

the girl and the boy   to the baby

a man and a woman   of the girl

to a boy and girl

Fluency Check Point *You have already listened to, practiced, and read the story. Read it again. Repeat until you not only get all the words right but you can also read it smoothly and with meaning.*

Evaluation *How do you think you did with this lesson? Listen to each statement. Then, color the face that best shows how you feel about your learning.*

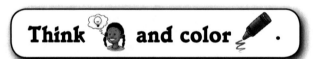

I know the words and phrases.

I can read the story.

I understand what naming words are.

I am learning to read.

Name _____ Date _____

Instant Words

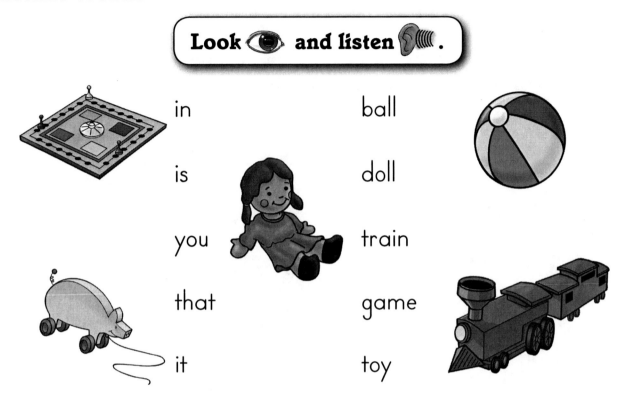

Look 👁 and listen 👂.

in	ball
is	doll
you	train
that	game
it	toy

Phrases

Read these phrases to yourself as you listen to them being read aloud.

Look 👁, listen 👂, and read 📖.

a toy	a ball	a toy train
a game	you see	in the train
a train	is it	that toy
a doll	it is	do you

Could you read every word? If not, repeat reading and listening until you can. Then, try reading the phrases on your own without listening.

Name _____ Date _____

Story *Read the story to yourself as you listen to it read aloud. Repeat reading and listening until you know every word.*

> **Look** 👁 **, listen** 👂 **, and read** 📖 **.**

You see a toy.

Is it a game?

It is a train.

It is a toy train.

A doll is in the train.

The doll has a ball.

I like that toy!

Do you like it?

About the Story *Finish each sentence with a group of words from the story.*

> **Look** 👁 **, listen** 👂 **, and write** ✏ **.**

1. You see a _____.

2. Is _____ a game?

3. A doll is _____ the train.

4. I like _____ toy!

Name _____ Date _____

On Your Own

Read 📖 and draw ✏️ .

a doll and a ball	you in a train
It is a game.	a toy that you like

Learning About Reading: *Word Order*

Listen 👂 .

You know the words it *and* is. *They are little words, but they are powerful. They often appear together. Let's make up some sentences with them. I'll start.* It is a game. It is a train. *Now you try.* It is_____. *I have some more.* It is Tuesday. It is warm. It is a good day to learn. *Who else has an "*It is*" sentence?*

Remember that we said that the words it *and* is *often appear together? What happens if we change the order? Let's make some sentences that begin with* Is it *instead of* It is. *I'll start again.* Is it a game? Is it a train? *What happens when these two little words trade places?*

Sentences that begin with It is *tell something. Sentences that begin with* Is it *ask something.*

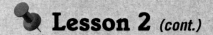

Name _____ Date _____

Try It! *Think about each sentence. Does it ask or tell? Use "Is it" if it asks, or "It is" if it tells.*

Think and write .

1. Is it a doll? _____ a doll.

2. _____ a game? It is a game.

3. Is it a train? _____ a train.

4. _____ a toy? It is a toy.

Fluency Checkpoint *You have already listened to and read the story. Read it again. Repeat until you not only get all the words right but you also can read it smoothly and with meaning.*

Read and repeat .

Evaluation *Did you learn to read in this lesson? Find out for yourself. Read the clues. Then, write the answer. It is a word from the story.*

Read and write .

It is a toy. Is it a train? It is not a train. Is it a ball? It is not a ball. Is it a game? It is not a game. It is a toy girl. Is it a doll?

It is a _____.

Name _____ Date _____

Instant Words

Look 👁 and listen 👂.

he   one

was   two

for   three

on   four

our   five

Phrases *Read these phrases to yourself as you listen to them being read aloud.*

Look 👁, listen 👂, and read 📖.

for you	on to the game	are you five
a boy was	four and two	four and one
he was	was he five	three and two
was he	he was five	three and three
are you	four and two	

Could you read every word? If not, repeat reading and listening until you can. Then, try reading the phrases on your own without listening.

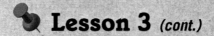

Lesson 3 *(cont.)*

Name _____ Date _____

Story *Read the story to yourself as you listen to it read aloud. Repeat reading and listening until you know every word.*

> **Look 👁 , listen 📢 , and read 📖 .**

It is a game for you.
A boy was three and two.
He was four and one.
Was he five?
He was five.
Are you on to the game?
You can play it.
What are you?
Are you five?
Are you three and three?
Are you four and two?

About the Story *Using the story, write the word that best completes each sentence.*

> **Look 👁 , read 📖 , and write ✏ .**

1. It is a _____ for you.

2. A boy was three and two. He was _____.

3. A girl was one and three. The girl was _____.

#50288–Increasing Fluency with High Frequency Word Phrases Grade 1 © Shell Education

Name _____ Date _____

On Your Own

Read 📖 and draw 🖍.

a game for you	a doll on a train
three balls and two balls	The baby was one.

Learning About Reading: *Prepositions*

Listen **.**

You have already learned that little words can have powerful meanings. Listen to these sentences:

The hat was on the baby.   **The hat was for the baby.**   **The hat was in the baby.**

These sentences have very different meanings, yet only one little word is different in each one. You already know these little words. They are on, for, and in. These words give us clues about what is coming next. Two more of these kinds of words that you already know are to and of.

When you see words such as these in a sentence, they signal that the next part of the sentence will tell you where, when, which, how, or why.

Let's make up some silly and not silly sentences using the words on, for, in, to, and of.

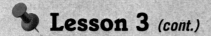

Name _____ Date _____

Try It! *Think about the "little words" we just discussed. Write the one that belongs in each sentence.*

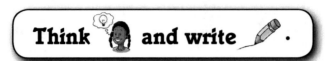

1. Give the ball ------------------- the baby.

2. One toy is ------------------- you.

3. He was ------------------- the train.

Fluency Checkpoint *You have already listened to, practiced, and read the story. Read the story again. Repeat until you not only get all the words right but you can also read it smoothly and with meaning.*

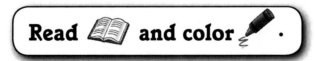

Evaluation *In the story of the three bears, Goldilocks tries each bear's porridge. She says one is too hot, one is too cold, and one is just right. Think about this lesson. Was it too hard, too easy, or just right for you? Color the face next to your choice.*

too hard   too easy   just right

Name _____ Date _____

Instant Words

Look 👁 and listen 👂.

as	shirt
with	pants
his	dress
they	shoes
I	hat

Phrases *Read these phrases to yourself as you listen to them being read aloud.*

Look 👁, listen 👂, and read 📖.

on a train	I am	with them
has on	the one	one of his shoes
a dress	in the hat	as they
pants and a shirt	they have	got on the train

Could you read every word? If not, repeat reading and listening until you can. Then, try reading the phrases on your own without listening.

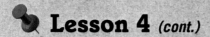

Name _____ Date _____

Story
Read the story to yourself as you listen to it being read aloud. Repeat reading and listening until you know every word.

> Look 👁 , listen 📢 , and read 📖 .

A man and a woman are **on a train.**

The man **has on pants and a shirt.**

The woman **has on a dress.**

I am the one in the hat.

They have a baby **with them.**

The baby lost **one of his shoes as they got on** the train.

About the Story
Finish each sentence with a group of words from the story.

> Look 👁 , listen 📢 , and write ✏ .

1. What does the man have on? _____

    _

2. What does the woman have on? _____

    _

3. What do I have on? _____

    _

4. What did the baby lose? _____

    _

5. Where did the baby lose it? _____

Name _____ Date _____

On Your Own

Read 📖 and draw ✏️ .

a dress and a hat	pants and a shirt
one of his shoes	I'm the one in the hat.

Learning About Reading: *Phrase Chunks*

Listen 👂 .

Listen again to this sentence: The baby lost one of his shoes as they got on the train. *That is a long sentence! Reading it all at once is like eating a whole big cookie in one bite. When you eat a big cookie, you break it apart into chunks first, and then eat one chunk at a time. Let's break the sentence up into chunks. (Write) The baby lost / one of his shoes / as they / got on the train. Who lost something? What did he lose? When did he lose it? Where did he lose it?*

We broke the sentence into four chunks, but not just anywhere. We broke it into meaningful groups of words. A meaningful group of words is called a phrase. Sentences, especially long ones, are easier to read and understand if you break them up into phrase chunks—meaningful groups of words. Are you ready to see how?

Lesson 4 *(cont.)*

Name _____ Date _____

Try It! *Each sentence below is shown in phrase chunks. Read the sentences in chunks. Then write the word that tells how many phrase chunks were in the sentence.*

1. The man has on / pants and a shirt. _____

2. I am the one / in the hat. _____

3. They have / a baby / with them. _____

4. The baby lost / one of his shoes / as they / got on the

    train. _____

Fluency Check Point *You have already listened to, practiced, and read the story. Read the story again. Repeat until you not only get all the words right but can also read it smoothly and with meaning.*

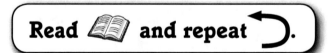

Evaluation *This lesson was about breaking up sentences into phrases—meaningful groups of words. Do you think that you understood the lesson? Find out. Draw a slanted line (/) in this sentence to break it into two meaningful phrase chunks.*

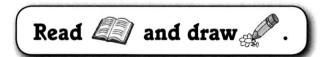

They dress the baby in a shirt and shoes.

#50288—Increasing Fluency with High Frequency Word Phrases Grade 1   © Shell Education

Name _____ Date _____

Instant Words

at	cat
be	dog
this	bird
have	fish
from	rabbit

Phrases *Read these phrases to yourself as you listen to them being read aloud.*

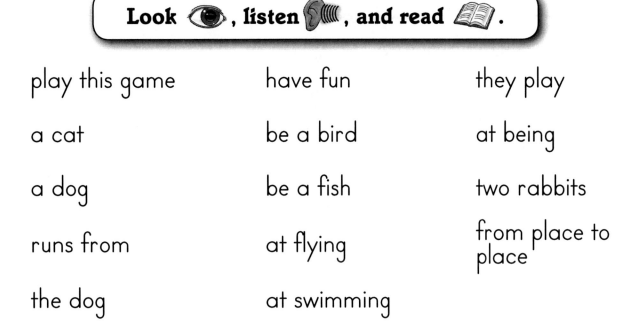

play this game	have fun	they play
a cat	be a bird	at being
a dog	be a fish	two rabbits
runs from	at flying	from place to place
the dog	at swimming	

Could you read every word? If not, repeat reading and listening until you can. Then, try reading the phrases on your own without listening.

Name _____ Date _____

Story *Read the story to yourself as you listen to it read aloud. Repeat reading and listening until you know every word.*

Look 👁 , listen 👂 , and read 📖 .

A girl and a boy **play this game.**
The girl is **a cat.** MEOW!
The boy is **a dog.** WOOF!
The cat **runs from the dog.**
They **have fun.**
Then, the girl can **be a bird.**
The boy can **be a fish.**
The girl plays **at flying.**
The boy plays **at swimming.**
Last, **they play at being two rabbits.**
They hop **from place to place.**

About the Story *Read the sentences. Write the word that finishes each sentence.*

Look 👁 , listen 👂 , and write ✏ .

1. The boy liked to be a _____ and a _____ .

2. The cat runs _____ the dog.

3. The girl and boy _____ fun.

Name _____ Date _____

On Your Own

> Read 📖 and draw ✏️ .

A girl and boy have fun at play.	The girl is a cat. MEOW!
The boy is a dog. WOOF!	They like to play this game.

Learning About Reading: *Getting the Sounds*

> Listen 👂 .

(Note: This lesson is on accuracy of ending sounds. Exaggerate the final sounds in the example words.) Close your eyes and listen to these two words very carefully: cat, rabbit. *Do they end with the same sound? How about* cat *and* bird? *What other words can you think of that end with the same sound as* cat?

Let's play a game. Close your eyes and don't open them. I'll say two words. If they end with the same sound, put up one hand. If they don't end with the same sound, don't put up your hand. Ready? this-dress, with-fish, five-have, with-this, was-as, on-one, dress-shoes, toy-boy, for-bird, from-fish, be-three, shirt-hat, you-shoes, are-four, rabbit-shirt. *(Note: As you say each pair, watch students' responses for accuracy. When you are finished, go back over each pair of words.)*

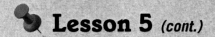

Lesson 5 (cont.)

Name _____ Date _____

Try It! Look at the first word in each row. Circle any word in the rest of the row that ends with the same sound as the first word. Be careful that you are matching sounds, not letters. Sometimes the letters may match, but not the sounds!

Think and circle.

this	dress	fish	pants	was
at	bird	hat	that	rabbit
be	five	game	three	they
have	of	five	baby	two
from	for	man	game	train

Fluency Checkpoint You have already listened to, practiced, and read the story. Read the story again. Repeat until you not only get all the words right but you can also read it smoothly and with meaning.

Read and repeat.

Evaluation Play this game with a partner. Pretend to be a dog and a cat. Then, pretend to be a bird and a fish. Last, pretend to be two rabbits hopping from place to place. Use words you know to write about it. Finish these sentences.

Read and write.

_____   _____

I was a _____ and a _____ .

_____

It was fun to be _____ .

Name _____ Date _____

Instant Words

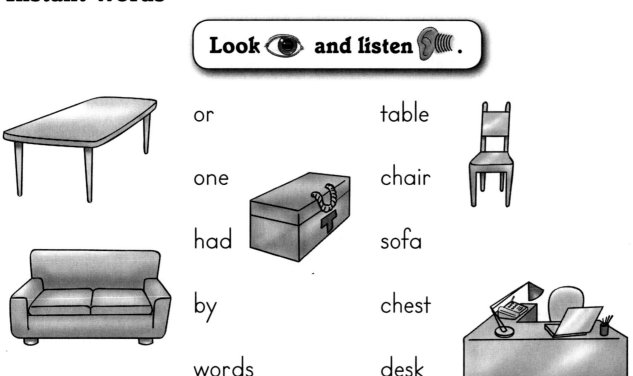

or   table

one   chair

had   sofa

by   chest

words   desk

Phrases *Read these phrases to yourself as you listen to them being read aloud.*

at the desk	had his toy ball	at the table
by the desk	by the toy chest	Fish for Words or Word Train
on the sofa	two word games	one or the other
under the table	on a chair	

Could you read every word? If not, repeat reading and listening until you can. Then, try reading the phrases on your own without listening.

Lesson 6 (cont.)

Name _____ Date _____

Story *Read the story to yourself as you listen to it read aloud. Repeat reading and listening until you know every word.*

> **Look 👁, listen 👂, and read 📖.**

Dad was **at the desk.**

The sofa is **by the desk.**

Mom was **on the sofa** with the baby.

The dog was **under the table.**

He **had his toy ball.**

The boy was **by the toy chest.**

He had **two word games.**

The girl was **on a chair at the table.**

The girl said, "Pick a game for you and me to play."

"Do you want to play **Fish for Words** or **Word Train?**

Pick **one or the other,**" he said.

The girl saw the dog with his ball.

"Let's go play ball with the dog!"

About the Story *Answer each question with a phrase from the story.*

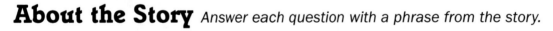

> **Look 👁, listen 👂, and write ✏.**

1. Where is Dad? _____

2. Where is Mom? _____

3. Where is the dog? _____

#50288–*Increasing Fluency with High Frequency Word Phrases Grade 1* © *Shell Education*

Name _____ Date _____

On Your Own

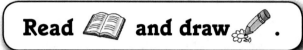

Read 📖 and draw ✏️ .

a ball on a chair	one sofa by a table
words on a shirt	a game in a toy chest

Learning About Reading: *Stress*

Listen 👂 .

Listen as I say this sentence three times (stress the underlined words): Dad *is at the desk. Dad* is *at the desk. Dad is at the* desk. *Did these sentences have any words that were different? No, but they sounded just a little bit different and had slightly different meanings. The difference was how I said the sentence. In each, I said a different word a little louder and stronger than the others. This is called stress.*

Saying something louder and stronger—stressing it—draws attention to the word. Think about the sentences again. I will ask you three questions. Each answer is the sentence Dad is at the desk. *Now see if you can figure out which word you would stress to answer each question. 1. Who is at the desk? (Dad) 2. Is Dad by the desk? (at) 3. Is Dad at the table? (desk)*

As you continue to get better and better at reading, you will find all kinds of uses for stressing words.

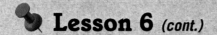

Name _____ Date _____

Try It! *Follow as each question is read. Read the answer to yourself. Then draw a line under the word that you would stress—say louder and stronger—in the answer.*

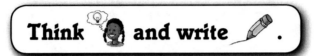

1. Was Mom on the sofa with the cat? Mom was on the sofa with the baby.

2. Who was by the toy chest? The boy was by the toy chest.

3. Was the dog on the table? The dog was under the table.

Fluency Checkpoint *You have already listened to, practiced, and read the story. Read it again. Repeat until you not only get all the words right but you also can read it smoothly and with meaning.*

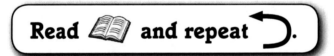

Evaluation *Work with a partner to see what you have learned. First, you read each question. Your partner reads the answer with one of the words stressed. Then, trade jobs.*

1. Is the <u>ball</u> in the toy chest? The game is in the toy chest.

2. Is the doll in the <u>toy chest</u>? The doll in is the chair.

Name _____ Date _____

Special Lesson: Group Choral Reading
Instant Words

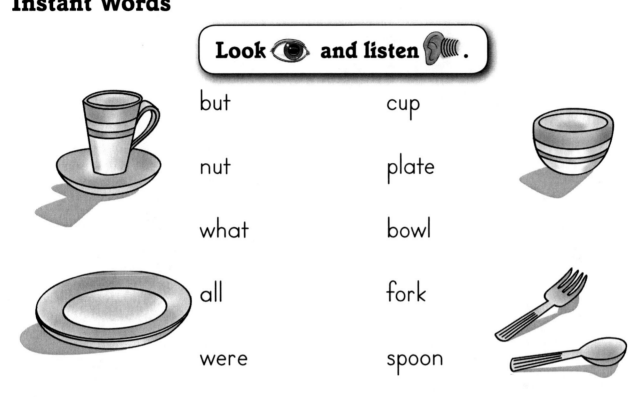

Look 👁 and listen 👂.	
but	cup
nut	plate
what	bowl
all	fork
were	spoon

Phrases *Read these phrases to yourself as you listen to them being read aloud.*

Look 👁, listen 👂, and read 📖.

a story about nuts	with cups, bowls, and plates	What were
read the words	forks and spoons	but what
all dressed up	but what they saw	so that all
they were ready	just one nut	they all sat down
table was set	all they had to eat	

Could you read every word? If not, repeat reading and listening until you can. Then, try reading the phrases on your own without listening.

Name _____ Date _____

Story *Read the story to yourself as you listen to it read aloud. Repeat reading and listening until you know every word.*

> **Look** 👁 **, listen** 👂 **, and read** 📖 **.**

This is **a story about nuts** and birds.

It is fun to **read the words.**

The birds came **all dressed up.**

They were ready for some supper.

The **table was set with cups, bowls, and plates.**

They picked up their **forks and spoons.**

But **what they saw** was **just one nut.**

That is **all they had to eat!**

What were they to do, **but what** they had to do?

They cut the one nut **so that all** had some.

Then, **they all sat down** and ate.

About the Story *Answer each question with a phrase from the story.*

> **Look** 👁 **, listen** 👂 **, and write** ✏ **.**

1. What is the story about? _____

_____

2. Who are **they** in the story? _____

_____

3. What was all that they had to eat? _____

Name _____ Date _____

On Your Own

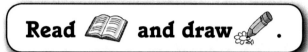
Read 📖 and draw ✏ .

birds all dressed up	a table set with a plate, a cup, a bowl
a bird with a fork and a spoon	just one nut on a plate

Learning About Reading: *Rhyming Sounds*

Listen 👂 .

Listen to these words: cat-hat, boy-toy, and-sand, and be-three. Do you know what we call these kinds of words? Rhyming words. Rhyming words are used in poems and songs. But, did you know that knowing rhyming words helps you read better? That is because if you can see a pattern in a word you know, you may be able to read a word you don't know that has the same pattern. Let's read again the first two lines of the story. Which words rhyme? Are they spelled alike or different?

Get ready to try to find words that rhyme. Remember that rhyming is something you hear, not see. In other words, two words may rhyme in sound, but not have the same letters.

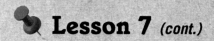

Name _____ Date _____

Try It! *Can you recognize words that rhyme? Read the word at the top of the list. Then, read the words under it. Circle any that rhyme with the word at the top.*

1. cup	2. plate	3. nut	4. words
up	they	ate	birds
supper	ate	but	were
cut	gate	up	forks
pup	sat	cut	or

Fluency Checkpoint (Choral Reading in Four Group Parts)

You will be given a part of the story to read aloud along with some classmates. Circle your group number. Study your part until you know it very well and can read it with meaning.

Group 1:   This is a story about nuts and birds.
           It is fun to read the words.

Group 2:   The birds came all dressed up.
           They were ready for some supper.
           The table was set with cups, bowls, and plates.

Group 3:   They picked up their forks and spoons.
           But what they saw was just one nut.
           That is all they had to eat!

Group 4:   What were they to do, but what they had to do?
           They cut the one nut so that all had some.
           Then, they all sat down and ate.

Evaluation *Think about how well you prepared and read your part of the story. Circle the number of stars that show what you think of your work.*

How I prepared ★★★ ★★ ★

How I read ★★★ ★★ ★

Name _____ Date _____

Special Lesson: Poetry for Shared Reading

Instant Words

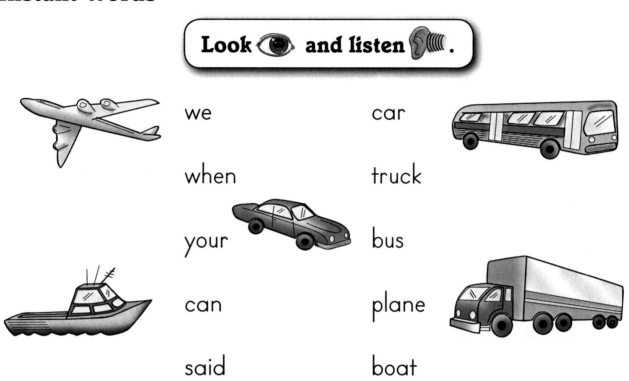

Look 👁 and listen 👂.

we   car

when   truck

your   bus

can   plane

said   boat

Phrases *Read these phrases to yourself as you listen to them being read aloud.*

Look 👁, listen 👂, and read 📖.

Mom said   your car   a truck can

when you   we can go   a boat or a plane

we can't go   on a bus   close your eyes

will we   in a truck

Could you read every word? If not, repeat reading and listening until you can. Then, try reading the phrases on your own without listening.

Name _____ Date _____

Poem (Poem for Shared Reading) *This is a special kind of poem meant to be read in parts. Where it says* **All**, *everyone reads together. Where you see an* **S**, *it means that the part is for students. Where you see a* **G**, *it is a part for a grown-up to read. Repeat reading and listening until you can read the part for All and each of the student (S) parts.*

> **Look 👁 , listen 👂 , and read 📖 .**

All:	"We'll go on a trip," **Mom said,**
	"**When you** are tucked in your bed."
S:	"**We can't go** on a trip from bed!"
G:	"We're just going in your head"
S:	"**Will we** drive and take **your car?**"
G:	"Only if it's not too far."
S:	"Well, **we can go on a bus.**"
G:	"No, I think it's too much fuss."
S:	"Then try our luck in **a truck?**"
G:	"**No, a truck** can get stuck."
S:	"How about **a boat or a plane?**"
G:	"Yes, a plane! Now, **close your eyes.**
	And dream of flying in the skies.

About the Poem *Finish each sentence with a word from the poem.*

> **Look 👁 , listen 👂 , and write ✏ .**

1. We'll go on a trip, Mom _____.

2. Now, close _____ eyes.

Name _____ Date _____

On Your Own

Read 📖 and draw ✏️ .

You are tucked into your bed.	You dream that you can fly a plane.

You close your eyes.

Learning About Reading: *Rhythm*

Listen 👂 .

A poem is a special kind of writing. It often has rhyming words. Where are the rhyming words in this poem? There's something else special about this poem. Two people are talking back and forth. That is called conversation. *Notice the marks before and after the words of whoever is speaking.*

We can't help but notice one other thing about this and many other poems. See if you can guess what it is. Listen to this: Teddy Bear, Teddy Bear Turn around. Teddy Bear, Teddy Bear spin in a circle and put your hands on the ground. That sounds silly, doesn't it? If you know the way it really goes, say it with me now: Teddy Bear, Teddy Bear Turn around. Teddy Bear, Teddy Bear touch the ground. Let's say it again. This time clap the beat as you say it. How many beats or claps are in each line? The pattern of beats is called rhythm. *Like music, many poems have rhythm. Let's read our poem again together and tap the beats as we read.*

Name _____   Date _____

Try It! *Below is a part of the poem you have been practicing. The parts that the grown-up reads have lines under the beats that are stressed. The parts that you read don't. Can you get the rhythm, and then draw lines under the stressed beats in your parts?*

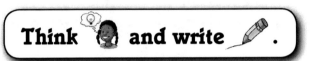

Think and write.

> "We're just going in your head."
> "Will we drive and take your car?"
> "Only if it's not too far."
> "Well, we can go on a bus."
> "No, I think it's too much fuss."
> "Then try our luck in a truck?"
> "No, a truck can get stuck."

Fluency Checkpoint: *Call and Response Shared Reading*
You have already listened to, practiced, and read the poem. Practice reading it again. Repeat until you not only get all the words right but you can also read it smoothly in rhythm as you do.

Read and repeat.

Evaluation *Ask a grown-up at home to read the poem with you. Tell the grown-up to read the parts marked with a **G**, and you read the parts marked with an **S**. Try reading it back and forth until you both get the rhythm. Then, read it one more time and clap or tap the rhythm as you do.*

1. I read the poem at home with _____ .

2. Did you get the rhythm? _____

3. Did the grown-up get the rhythm? _____

Name _____ Date _____

Instant Words

Look 👁 and listen 👂.

there   bread

use   meat

an   soup

each   apple

which   cereal

Phrases *Read these phrases to yourself as you listen to them being read aloud.*

Look 👁, listen 👂, and read 📖.

there are	bowl of cereal	bread and meat
from which to choose	cup of soup	an apple
use your	use some	each of these

Could you read every word? If not, repeat reading and listening until you can. Then, try reading the phrases on your own without listening.

Name _____ Date _____

Story
Read the story to yourself as you listen to it read aloud. Repeat reading and listening until you know every word.

> **Look** 👁 **, listen** 👂 **, and read** 📖 **.**

When you want a snack, **there are** many foods **from which to choose.**
Use your head. Pick foods that are good for you.
You can have a **bowl of cereal** or a **cup of soup.**
Use some bread and meat to make a sandwich.
Have **an apple** or some nuts.
Each of these foods is good for you.

About the Story
Below are questions about the story. Each question has three answer choices. Follow as the question is read. Read the answers. Then color in the circle of your choice.

> **Listen** 👂 **, read** 📖 **, and color** ✏ **.**

Example: What should you use when you pick a food for a snack?
○ an apple   ● your head   ○ bread and meat

1. Which of these is the best title for this story?
○ Good For You   ○ Have a Snack   ○ A Bowl of Cereal

2. Which of these is not a food?
○ soup   ○ apple   ○ each

3. Which of these do you use to make a sandwich?
○ cereal and a bowl   ○ meat and bread   ○ soup and an apple

#50288—Increasing Fluency with High Frequency Word Phrases Grade 1

Name _____ Date _____

On Your Own   *The story told you which foods were good for you. In each box below draw and label a food that is good for you.*

Draw 🖍️ and write ✏️ .

Each of these is good for you.

Learning About Reading: *Chunking for Smoothness*

Listen 👂 .

Do you remember what you learned about breaking up sentences into chunks—meaningful groups of words? Let's break up the first long sentence of the story into chunks so that it is easier to read.

When you want a snack, / there are many foods / from which to choose.

Does it matter where you break a sentence? Yes. Here is the same sentence, but broken into different chunks.

When you want a / snack, there are / many foods from / which to choose.

Chunking it this way makes it harder to read and understand. The trick is to chunk groups of words that make sense together. Try reading the following sentence chunked in two different ways, and see which way makes the most sense.

I ate / a bowl of cereal.   I ate a bowl / of cereal.

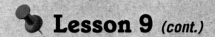

Name _____ Date _____

Try It! *Here are some phrase chunks from the story. Can you match the chunks to form sentences that make sense? Draw a line from each phrase on the left to one on the right. Form sentences that makes sense.*

Have an apple   is good for you.

Use your head   or some nuts.

Make a sandwich   to pick foods.

Each of these   with some bread and meat.

Fluency Checkpoint *You have already listened to, practiced, and read the story. Read it again. Repeat until you can get all the words right and read it smoothly and with meaning.*

Evaluation *Are you reading word-by-word or in chunks? Test your own chunking power! Here is a sentence chunked two different ways. Which way makes sense? Circle number #1 or #2.*

1. You can / have a bowl of / cereal or / some soup.

2. You can have / a bowl of cereal / or some soup.

#50288—Increasing Fluency with High Frequency Word Phrases Grade 1   © *Shell Education*

Name _____ Date _____

Instant Words

Look 👁 and listen 👂.

she   water

do   milk

how   juice

their   soda

if   tea

Phrases *Read these phrases to yourself as you listen to them being read aloud.*

Look 👁, listen 👂, and read 📖.

she and the doll	poured their tea	some juice
a tea party	real tea	will do
how do you like	she said	their tea
your tea	if you	their party
do you want milk	how about	

Could you read every word? If not, repeat reading and listening until you can. Then, try reading the phrases on your own without listening.

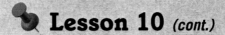

Name _____ Date _____

Story
Read the story to yourself as you listen to it read aloud. Repeat reading and listening until you know every word.

Look 👁 , listen 👂 , and read 📖 .

A girl played with her doll.

She and the doll had a tea party.

The girl set the table.

The doll sat in a chair.

The girl said, "How do you like your tea?"

"Do you want milk in it?"

The girl poured their tea.

It was not real tea. It was just water.

Then she said, "If you don't want tea, how about some juice?"

The girl said the words for the doll.

"This will do just fine."

So they had their tea and their party.

About the Story
Did you understand the story? Complete each sentence.

Look 👁 , read 📖 , and write ✏ .

1. In the story, the girl played with _____ .
_____

2. The girl asked, "_____ want milk in it?"
_____   _____

3. At the end, they had _____ tea and _____ party.
_____   _____

Name _____ Date _____

On Your Own

Read 📖 and draw ✏️ .

She poured the tea.	She sat in a chair.
She asked, "How do you like your tea?"	They had their tea party.

Learning About Reading: *Sound-Alikes*

Listen  .

Say these two words: there *and* their. *What do you notice about them? They sound exactly the same! But, they have different spellings and different meanings. Reading is not just saying the words correctly. It means understanding what you read as well. Here are two sentences.* There *is a cup of tea. It is* their *tea party. In the first sentence, the word* there—*t-h-e-r-e—means "in that place." In the second sentence the word* their—*t-h-e-i-r—means "belongs to them."*

Here's a trick for remembering which is which. There *means "in that place." The word* here *means "a place." You can see the word* here *in* there.

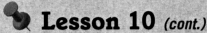

Name _____ Date _____

Try It! *You learned that the words* there *and* their *sound the same, but they have different spellings and different meanings. Complete each sentence with the correct form of the word.*

Think and write .

1. The girls played with _____ dolls.

2. "Put the tea cups _____ on the table," said a girl.

3. " _____ is milk and juice, too," she said.

4. The girls and _____ dolls had fun playing tea party.

Fluency Checkpoint *You have already listened to, practiced, and read the story. Read it again. Repeat until you can get all the words right and read it smoothly and with meaning.*

Read and repeat .

Evaluation *Think about how much you are learning about words and reading. Below are some of the things you have been learning. Which is hardest for you? easiest? in between? Follow as they are read to you. Then, write a number **1** on the line before the easiest thing for you. Write a **3** on the line before the hardest thing for you. Write a **2** before the thing that is in between easiest and hardest.*

_____ Learning to read and remember new words.

_____ Reading and understanding the stories.

_____ Learning about how to read, such as chunking.

Name _____ Date _____

Instant Words

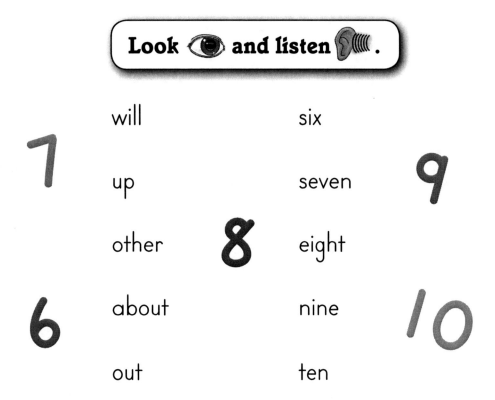

Look 👁 and listen 👂.

7 will   six
up   seven 9
other 8 eight
6 about   nine 10
out   ten

Phrases *Read these phrases to yourself as you listen to them being read aloud.*

Look 👁, listen 👂, and read 📖.

it will be	out in the yard	will begin
I am six	up to nine or ten	about eight o'clock
about to be seven	other than me	Will you come?

Could you read every word? If not, repeat reading and listening until you can. Then, try reading the phrases on your own without listening.

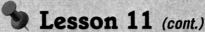

Name _____ Date _____

Story *Read the story to yourself as you listen to it being read aloud. Repeat reading and listening until you know every word.*

> **Look** 👁 , **listen** 👂 , **and read** 📖 .

Soon **it will** be my birthday.

I **am six** now, but I am **about to be seven.**

Dad said that I can have a party **out in the yard.**

I can have **up to nine or ten** boys and girls **(other than** me).

The party **will begin about eight o'clock** on Saturday.

Will you come?

About the Story *Did you understand the story? Complete each sentence.*

> **Look** 👁 , **read** 📖 , **and write** ✏ .

1. What will it be soon? _____
   _____

2. How old will I be? _____
   _____

3. Where will the party be? _____
   _____

4. When will the party begin? _____

Name _____ Date _____

Learning About Reading: *Sentence or Phrase?*

You have learned that a group of meaningful words is called a phrase. Here is an example:

out in the yard

Now, think about two cakes. One is whole and complete. The other has a missing slice; it is incomplete. The incomplete one is still a cake, but it is missing a part. A phrase is like the incomplete cake. It still has meaning, but it is not a complete thought.

A sentence is also a group of meaningful words. But, like a whole cake, a sentence is a complete thought. Here is an example:

The party will be out in the yard.

On Your Own *Read each group of words. Is it a sentence—a complete thought? Or is it a phrase—an incomplete thought? Put a check mark √ under the correct column. The first two are done for you to show you how.*

Read 📖 , think 💭👧 , and check √.

Group of Words	Sentence (whole)	Phrase (part)
out in the yard		√
The party will be out in the yard.	√	
1. other than me		
2. I will have a party.		
3. about eight o'clock		
4. up to nine or ten		
5. Sit in the other chair.		
6. with a ball		
7. out of time		
8. There are seven toys.		

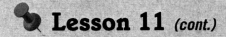
Name _____ Date _____

Try It! *You have learned the difference between a phrase and a sentence. A phrase is just a meaningful group of words. A sentence is a whole, complete thought. But, there's another difference. Sentences look different from phrases. Go back and look again at the chart you completed. Notice that each group of words that is a sentence begins with a capital letter. Fill in the missing letter in each sentence below.*

A sentence is a whole, complete thought. Every sentence begins with a capital letter.

> **Think and write .**

I or i   _____ will have a party.

S or s   _____ it in the other chair.

T or t   _____ here are seven toys.

Fluency Checkpoint *You have already listened to, practiced, and read the story. Read it again. Repeat until you can get all the words right and read it smoothly and with meaning.*

> **Read and repeat .**

Evaluation *Below are three phrases. To see if you understood this lesson, pick one of the phrases to make into a whole sentence. Write or dictate your sentence. Then answer the questions.*

Phrases: **at ten o'clock   in and out   up to seven**

_____

_____

Is your sentence a complete thought?   ☺ ☹

Does your sentence begin with a capital letter?   ☺ ☹

Name _____ Date _____

Instant Words

Look 👁 and listen 👂.

many	fruit
then	orange
them	grape
these	pear
so	banana

Phrases
Read these phrases to yourself as you listen to them being read aloud.

Look 👁, listen 👂, and read 📖.

Do you like fruit?	Do you like grapes?	have fruit
many fruits	don't like them	don't like fruit
eat a banana	grape juice	then you can
eat a pear or an orange	eating fruit	have fruit juice
these are	so, you should	

Could you read every word? If not, repeat reading and listening until you can. Then, try reading the phrases on your own without listening.

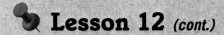
Name _____ Date _____

Story
Read the story to yourself as you listen to it read aloud. Repeat reading and listening until you know every word.

Look 👁 , listen 👂 , and read 📖 .

Do you like fruit? I like many fruits.

I **eat a banana** before school.

I **eat a pear or an orange** after school.

These are my favorites.

Do you like grapes? I **don't like them,** but I like **grape juice.**

Eating fruit is good for you.

So, you should have fruit every day.

If you **don't like fruit,** then you can **have fruit juice.**

Doesn't that sound good?

About the Story
Follow along as the questions are read to you. Then, answer the questions with words from the story.

Look 👁 , read 📖 , and write ✏ .

1. What are my favorite fruits?

   _____

   _____

2. What fruit don't I like?

   _____

   _____

3. When should you have fruit?

   _____

Name _____ Date _____

On Your Own

> ## Read 📖 and draw ✏️.

There are some fruits in a bowl.	This is a banana and an orange.
These are some grapes.	I see them, and then I eat them!

Learning About Reading: *Pitch*

> ## Listen .

Below are two sentences from the story. Pretend you are a robot and read them like a robot would sound—with no change in your voice.

I like many fruits. Do you like fruit?

Imagine if we all read like robots. It would be really boring. Now, read the sentences again—this time like humans. When you read like a human instead of a robot, your voice changes at the end of each sentence. It goes up or down a little. As you read the sentences again, trace a line in the air that follows your voice. The first sentence is a telling sentence. It ends with a period. Did your voice go up or down at the end? The second sentence is an asking sentence. It ends with a question mark. What happened to your voice at the end of the question?

A telling sentence ends with a period. At the end of a telling sentence, your voice goes down. An asking sentence ends with a question mark. At the end of a question your voice goes up.

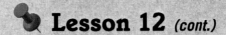

Name _____ Date _____

Try It! *Some of the sentences below are telling sentences and some are asking sentences. Read each sentence. Think about how your voice goes at the end of the sentence. Then draw an UP arrow or a DOWN arrow to show if your voice goes up or down.*

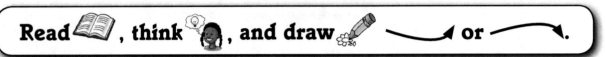

1. The fruit is in a bowl.

2. What is your favorite fruit?

3. I like grapes.

4. Can we make some orange juice?

5. When do you have fruit?

6. Fruit can be good on cereal.

Fluency Checkpoint *You have already listened to, practiced, and read the story. Read it again. Repeat until you can get all the words right and read it smoothly and with meaning.*

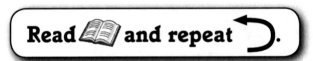

Evaluation *Do you read like a robot or do you make your voice go up and down to show expression? Read these two sentences to a partner. Have your partner listen and then tell you if your voice sounded the same or changed at the end of each sentence.*

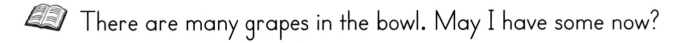 There are many grapes in the bowl. May I have some now?

My partner says that my voice sounded _____ at the end of each sentence.

Name _____ Date _____

Instant Words

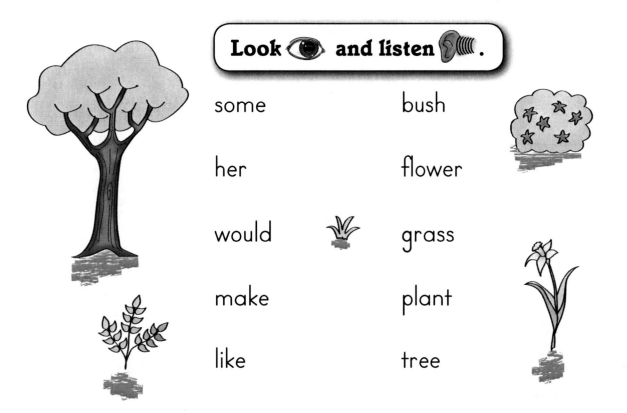

Look 👁 and listen 👂.

some	bush
her	flower
would	grass
make	plant
like	tree

Phrases Read these phrases to yourself as you listen to them being read aloud.

Look 👁, listen 👂, and read 📖.

in her chair	a plant	would make a nice home
her yard	only grass	that would make me happy
no flowers or trees	would like to have	so, the woman got up
no bushes	plant some bushes	out of her chair

Could you read every word? If not, repeat reading and listening until you can. Then, try reading the phrases on your own without listening.

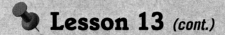

Name _____ Date _____

Story *Read the story to yourself as you listen to it read aloud. Repeat reading and listening until you know every word.*

> **Look 👁 , listen 👂 , and read 📖 .**

A woman sat outside **in her chair.**

She looked around **her yard.**

There were **no flowers or trees.**

There were **no bushes.**

There wasn't even **a plant.**

There was **only grass.**

"I **would like to have** a garden," she said.

"I could **plant some bushes,** flowers, and trees.

A garden **would make a nice home** for the birds.

That would make me happy, too!"

So, **the woman got up out of her chair** and began to plan her garden.

About the Story *Answer each question with a phrase from the story.*

> **Look 👁 , read 📖 , and write ✏ .**

1. Where did the woman sit? _____

2. What was in her yard? _____

3. What did she want to plant? _____

4. How would that make her feel? _____

Name _____ Date _____

On Your Own

Read 📖 and draw ✏️ .

1. This is where the woman sat.	2. This is what was in the yard.

3. This is what she wants to make.

Learning About Reading: *Stopping for Periods*

Listen 👂 .

Why do you think there are stop signs on streets? What would happen if there were none? All the cars, trucks, and even bikes would run together, get tangled up, and no one would be able to get where they were going!

In reading, the period (.) is like a stop sign at the end of a telling sentence. When you are reading, the period is the signal for the end of the thought. If you are reading aloud, you already know how your voice sounds when you come to a period in a telling sentence. Your voice goes down a little at the end. The period not only gives you the chance to breathe, but also to take a peek at what is coming next. This helps you read smoothly and keeps you from getting tangled up in words!

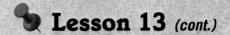

Lesson 13 (cont.)

Name _____ Date _____

Try It! *In each line below there are two sentences. But the periods are missing. Can you tell where the first complete thought ends? That's where the period belongs. Remember, a period is like a stop sign at the end of a telling sentence. Add the periods to these pairs of sentences.*

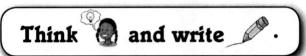

1. She made a garden It had bushes

2. There was grass and some trees There were some flowers

3. The garden was nice for the birds It made the woman happy

4. She liked her garden She liked to sit in her chair in her garden

Fluency Checkpoint *You have already listened to, practiced, and read the story. Read it again. Use what you know about periods to read the sentences. Repeat reading the story until you not only get all the words right but you also can read it smoothly and with meaning.*

Evaluation *Follow along as each statement is read. Think about your own learning. Color in the happy face if your answer is **yes**, and the unhappy face if your answer is **no**.*

I am learning to read smoothly.		
Learning about sentences helps me to read better.		
I understand what periods are for.		

#50288–Increasing Fluency with High Frequency Word Phrases Grade 1   © Shell Education

Name _____ Date _____

Instant Words

Look 👁 and listen 👂.

him	sun
into	moon
time	star
has	cloud
look	rain

Phrases *Read these phrases to yourself as you listen to them being read aloud.*

Look 👁, listen 👂, and read 📖.

has pictures	with him	of stars
to look at	of a cloud	the sun is a star
Oh, look!	clouds are	of the moon
into the room	of raindrops	moon is full
to him	it rains	than the sun

Could you read every word? If not, repeat reading and listening until you can. Then, try reading the phrases on your own without listening.

Name _____ Date _____

Story *Read the story to yourself as you listen to it read aloud. Repeat reading and listening until you know every word.*

Look 👁 , listen 👂 , and read 📖 .

Miss Lee said, "It is time for science. A scientist is coming.

He **has pictures** for you **to look at.** They are of things in the sky.

Oh, **look!** Here he is now."

The man came **into the room.** We said "Hi" **to him.**

The man did have pictures **with him.**

He had a picture **of a cloud.**

He said that **clouds are** made **of raindrops.**

When the clouds get full, **it rains.**

He had pictures **of stars.** He said that **the sun is a star!**

He had pictures **of the moon.**

He said that when the **moon is full,** it looks big, but it is smaller **than the sun.**

We liked the man. We learned many things **from him.**

About the Story *Listen as the questions and answer choices are read. Think about the story. Then circle the best answer.*

Listen 👂 , think 🧑 , and (circle) .

1. Who is Miss Lee?   a scientist   a teacher

2. What are raindrops made of?   water   clouds

3. Which is a star?   the moon   the sun

Name _____ Date _____

On Your Own

Read 📖 and draw ✏️ .

Rain comes from clouds.	There are many stars in the sky.
The sun is a star.	The moon looks big when it is full.

Learning About Reading: *Word Variants*

Listen 👂 .

You know how to read a lot more words than you think you do! That's because when you know one word, you may already know more. Here's proof! The first word below is one you know—rain. If you know the word rain, you can figure out other words that are made from it.

rain   **rains**   **raining**   **rained**   **rainy**

Notice that all the new words were made by adding endings to the word you already knew—rain.
You could read them all, couldn't you? You are ready to try some on your own.

Name _____   Date _____

Try It! *First, look at how a new word is made from a word you know. Write the new word in the sentence. Then read the sentence.*

Look 👁 , write ✏ , and read 📖 .

1. rain + y = rainy   It is a _____ day.

2. like + s = likes   He _____ to play games.

3. do + ing = doing   What are you _____ ?

4. look + ed = looked   We _____ at his pictures.

Fluency Checkpoint *You have already listened to, practiced, and read the story. Read it again. Repeat until you can get all the words right and read it smoothly and with meaning.*

Read 📖 and repeat ↩ .

Evaluation *In this lesson you discovered that if you can read a word, you can also read other words made from it. You already know the words* look, rain, cloud, *and* sun. *Show yourself how much you have learned! Choose one of the words below. Write a sentence with it.*

| looking | rained | cloudy | sunny |

_____

_____

_____

_____ .

Name _____ Date _____

Special Lesson: Reading and Following Directions
Instant Words

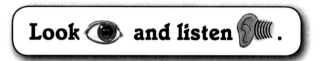

two	lake
more	rock
write	dirt
go	field
see	hill

Phrases *Read these phrases to yourself as you listen to them being read aloud.*

a small lake	the sun and a cloud	a big rock
some dirt	draw a hill	two more
around the lake	make a field	in the field
go to	next to the hill	write an X
the top	the bottom	hard to see

Could you read every word? If not, repeat reading and listening until you can. Then, try reading the phrases on your own without listening.

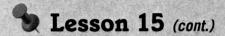

Name _____ Date _____

Directions *In this lesson, you are not reading a story. You are going to read and follow directions to make a treasure map. Read the directions to yourself as you listen to them being read aloud. Repeat reading and listening until you know every word.*

Look 👁, listen 👂, and read 📖.

This is how to make a treasure map.

Draw a **small lake** in the middle of the map. Put **some dirt around the lake.**

Go to **the top** of the map. Put **the sun and a cloud** in the sky.

Draw a **hill. Make a field next** to the hill.

Go to **the bottom** of the map. Draw two trees.

Put **a big rock** under one of the trees. Draw **two more** trees **in the field.**

Write an X on the map where the treasure is hidden.

Make it small so that it is **hard to see.**

About the Directions *Listen to the questions as they are read to you. Answer them with words from the directions.*

Look 👁, listen 👂, and write ✏.

1. What is in the middle of the map? _____

2. What is in the sky? _____

3. How many trees in all? _____

4. How big should you write the X? _____

Name _____ Date _____

On Your Own and Learning About Reading: *Directions*

Listen 🔊, read 📖, and draw ✏️.

Directions tell you how to do something. They use direction words, such as write, draw, *and* find. *These words tell you what to do. You have listened to and read the directions for making a treasure map. Now it is your turn to try it. Read and follow the directions to make a map in the box below.*

This is how to make a treasure map.

Draw a small lake in the middle of the map. Put some dirt around the lake.

Go to the top of the map. Put the sun and a cloud in the sky.

Draw a hill. Make a field next to the hill.

Go to the bottom of the map. Draw two trees.

Put a big rock under one of the trees. Draw two more trees in the field.

Write an X on the map where the treasure is hidden.

Make it small so that it is hard to see.

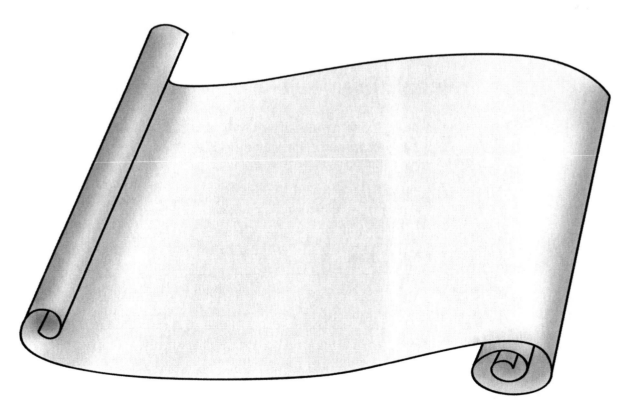

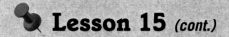

Name _____ Date _____

Try It! and Fluency Checkpoint *In this lesson you practiced reading and following directions. Find out how well you are doing. Below are some questions and a map. Read each question. Use the map to find the answer. Then, answer yes or no.*

Read 📖 and write ✏ yes or no.

1. Do you see two lakes? _____

2. Are there more rocks than trees? _____

3. Are all of the hills the same size? _____

4. Do you see rocks in the field? _____

5. Are there more than two clouds in the sky? _____

Evaluation *Reading directions carefully is an important skill you will use for the rest of your life. Find out how well someone can follow directions that you read aloud. Ask someone at home to help you. Your helper will need a blank sheet of paper and a pencil. Tell your helper that you are going to read some directions for making a map. Your helper is to see if he or she can follow them by doing what you read. Then, fill in the line below with the name of your helper.*

I read the directions to

_____

_____

_____ .

Name _____   Date _____

Instant Words *Read these phrases to yourself as you listen to them read aloud.*

Look 👁 and listen 👂.

number	horse
no	cow
way	pig
could	chicken
people	duck

Phrases *Read these phrases to yourself as you listen to them being read aloud.*

Look 👁, listen 👂, and read 📖.

there could be	a number of other	you could have
a long way	fields of grass	any number
cows, chickens, and pigs	trees to climb	your own horse
a lake with ducks		

Could you read every word? If not, repeat reading and listening until you can. Then, try reading the phrases on your own without listening.

Name _____ Date _____

Story *Read the story to yourself as you listen to it read aloud. Repeat reading and listening until you know every word.*

Look 👁 , listen 👂 , and read 📖 .

Would you like to live on a farm?

There could be more animals than people.

You would have to go **a long way** to school.

There could be no boys or girls to play with nearby.

But, if you lived on a farm, you would not be alone.

There could be cows, chickens, and pigs.

There might be **a lake with ducks** and **a number of** other birds.

On a farm, you might have **fields of grass** to play in and **trees to climb.**

You could have any number of pets.

You might even have **your own horse!**

About the Story *This story gave some reasons that you might like living on a farm and reasons you might not like it. Think about the question: Would you like to live on a farm? Write one phrase telling what you might like about it, and one telling what you might not like about it.*

Think 💭 and write ✏️ .

_____

1. I would like _____ .

_____

2. I would not like _____ .

Name _____ Date _____

On Your Own
In the box below, draw a farm scene and label these things: a field of grass, cows on a hill, trees, ducks on a lake, a horse, and some pigs.

Learning About Reading: *Sound and Sense*

> ### Listen 👂 .

There are thousands of different words. The good news is that you don't have to learn them all one by one. Sometimes when you come to a word you don't know, you can use a trick called "sound and sense" to help you figure it out. Here's how it works. Pretend that you are reading this sentence and you come to a word you don't know—the one in dark print:

> *On a farm, you could* **feed** *bread to the ducks in the lake.*

First, look at the word. Think about the words around it. Ask yourself what the sentence is about and what you already know. In this case, you know it is about ducks in a lake on a farm. You know the word bread. *So what word would make sense in the sentence? You think of the word* give. *You* could *give bread to the ducks. That word does make sense. But is it the right word?*

Next, look at the word again. This time look at the letters and think of the sounds of the letters. The word begins with f and the f-sound. Does your word, give, begin with the f-sound? No, so that can't be the right word. Go back to the sentence and try to think of another word that would make sense and *begins with the f-sound. It ends with the d-sound. Then it comes to you! Feed! You could feed bread to the ducks. The word* feed *has the right sounds and makes sense.*

Name _____ Date _____

Try It! *You learned a trick for figuring out what a word you don't know might be. The trick is called "sound and sense." Below are some sentences. One word in each sentence does not make sense. Draw a line through it. Then, think of a word you know that does make sense there. Write it on the line.*

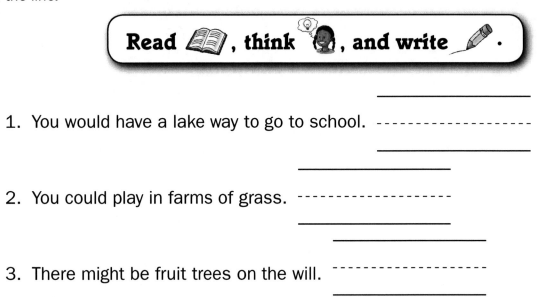

1. You would have a lake way to go to school. - - - - - - - - - - - - - - - - -
   _____

2. You could play in farms of grass. - - - - - - - - - - - - - - - - -
   _____
   _____

3. There might be fruit trees on the will. - - - - - - - - - - - - - - - - -
   _____

Fluency Checkpoint *You have already listened to, practiced, and read the story. Read it again. Repeat until you can get all the words right and read it smoothly and with meaning.*

Evaluation *Think about your reading and how you feel about what you are learning. Follow along as each statement is read to you. Then underline YES if you think it is true for you. Underline NO if you think it is not true for you.*

I sometimes read the wrong word.   YES NO

I know when I have read a word wrong because it doesn't make sense. YES   NO

I guess at words I don't know or am unsure of.   YES   NO

I understand how to figure out new words using Sound and Sense. YES NO

Name _____ Date _____

Special Lesson: Reading a Letter
Instant Words

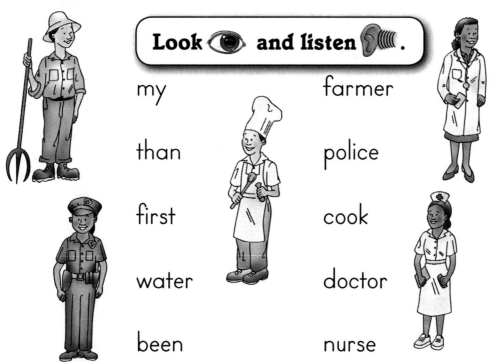

Look and listen.

my	farmer
than	police
first	cook
water	doctor
been	nurse

Phrases *Read these phrases to yourself as you listen to them being read aloud.*

Look , listen , and read .

my first day	colder than	a doctor
but first	a farmer	a nurse!
the water	a cook	to cook my dinner
was cold	with the police	will write

Could you read every word? If not, repeat reading and listening until you can. Then, try reading the phrases on your own without listening.

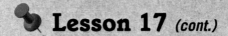
Name _____ Date _____

Story *Read the letter to yourself as you listen to it read aloud. Repeat reading and listening until you know every word.*

Dear Grandma,

It is **my first day** at summer camp. There are many things to do. **But first,** we got to get in the lake. It was a hot day, but **the water was cold!** When I got out, I was **colder than** I am in winter! I have been trying to get warm again all day.

Some of the boys' fathers came to camp with us. On the bus they were telling us about their jobs. One dad is **a farmer.** One is **a cook.** When one dad said that he was **with the police,** we all said "Uh-oh!" Another dad is **a doctor** and one is even **a nurse!**

I have to go now. It is time **to cook my dinner. I will write** more soon.

Love,

Chris

About the Story *You will not be writing the answers to the questions below, but you will still be asked for answers. Listen as each question about the letter is read to you. Think about the question. Then, be ready to offer your ideas in a class discussion.*

1. Is Chris a boy or a girl? How do you know?

2. What word used in the story means "belongs to me"?

3. Up and down, big and little, first and last—these are all opposites. Can you find two pairs of opposites used in the letter?

Name _____ Date _____

On Your Own

Read 📖 and draw ✏️

The water in the lake is cold!	One dad was a cook. One was a nurse.
One dad was with the police. "Uh-oh!"	I am cooking my dinner at summer camp.

Learning About Reading: *Comparing Words*

Listen 👂.

Think of something big—like a car. Then, think about a bus. Compare the car and the bus. How would you finish this sentence: A bus is _____ than a car. Now, think about a plane. Compare the size of all three. Finish this sentence: A plane is _____ of all.

When you were comparing the size of two things, you changed the word big *to* bigger *and used the word* than. *When you compared three things, you changed* big *to* biggest *and used the words* of all. *The words* big, bigger, *and* biggest *are called comparing words. Here's a trick for recognizing comparing words. If two things are being compared, you will often see the ending -er on the comparing word followed by the word* than. *If three or more things are being compared, you will often see the ending -est on the comparing word.*

Here are some examples: big/bigger/biggest, cold/colder/coldest, warm/warmer/warmest

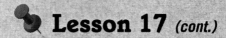

Name _____ Date _____

Try It! *In this lesson you learned about comparing words. One of the words below is often used when comparing two things. The other one means when. Time to check your memory and reading power. Fill in the words where they belong in the sentences below.*

> Listen 👂, think 🧑, and write ✏️ then or than.

I had some cereal and --------------------- some juice.

The juice was colder --------------------- the milk.

Fluency Checkpoint *You have already listened to, practiced, and read the story. Read it again. Repeat until you can get all the words right and read it smoothly and with meaning.*

> Read 📖 and repeat ↩️

Evaluation *Think about how well you are learning to read and all the new things you know about words and how they work. Below are three of the things you have been learning and three comparison words. After they are read to you, write one of the comparing words in front of each thing to show how you feel about it*

hard   **harder**   **hardest**

_____
-------------------------- Learning to read and remember new words
_____
_____
-------------------------- Reading and understanding the stories
_____
_____
-------------------------- Learning about how to read, such as recognizing
_____ comparing words

Name _____ Date _____

Instant Words

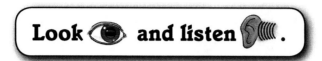

called   television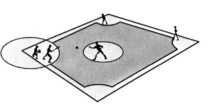

who   radio

   oil   movie

sit   ball game

now   band

Phrases *Read these phrases to yourself as you listen to them being read aloud.*

in the band	on the radio	sit down
at ball games	called to me	is on now
on television	right now	whom do you see

Could you read every word? If not, repeat reading and listening until you can. Then, try reading the phrases on your own without listening.

Name _____ Date _____

Story
Read the story to yourself as you listen to it read aloud. Repeat reading and listening until you know every word.

> **Look 👁 and read 📖 .**

Bill is my big brother. He is in college.

He plays **in the band**. The band plays **at ball games**.

Sometimes the games are **on television**.

Sometimes they are **on the radio**.

One Saturday, I was out in the yard.

Dad was inside watching the game.

Suddenly, he **called to me**. "Quick! Come **right now!**

Come in and **sit down**. The band **is on now!**"

I came in and sat down.

Dad said, "Look! **Whom do you see?**"

I looked. I looked some more. Then, I saw him.

There was my brother Bill **on television!**

About the Story
Listen as each question is read. Then, answer with words from the story.

> **Look 👁 , listen 👂 , and write ✏ .**

1. Who is in college? _____

2. Where does the band play? _____

3. When was Bill on television? _____

Name _____ Date _____

On Your Own *Read the story again. Think about what happened first, next, and last. In the three boxes below, draw what happened first, next, and last.*

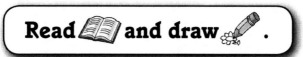

First	Next	Last

Learning About Reading: *Exclamations!*

Look at these sentences from the story: Bill is my big brother. Quick! Come right now!

First, read them both like a robot—with no feeling or expression. Now, read them again—this time as a <u>person</u> would—with human feelings and expression.

When Dad said, "Quick! Come right now!" was he bored? mad? excited? Try reading his words now as if he was bored. Now read the same words as if he was mad. Finally, read them as if he was excited. You can see that HOW you read the words makes a big difference in showing the meaning and feeling of the words. A good reader, like you, doesn't sound like a robot. You think about what feelings the words are expressing and use your voice to show those feelings.

Look at Dad's words again. Notice that a special mark is used (!). This mark, called an exclamation mark, is a signal that the words express strong feeling.

Name _____ Date _____

Try It! *You are a person, not a robot, so you should read like a person, not a robot. When you read, you should not only think about what the words are, but also about what feelings the words are showing. Practice reading sentences with strong feeling. Remember that the ! is your signal that the words express strong feeling. Say them a little louder and quicker.*

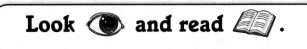

Look 👁 and read 📖.

1. She saw the bus coming. "Look out!" she called to the boy.

2. It was a hot day, but the water was cold!

3. Bill called to his dog, "Come here right now!"

4. "Wow! I got first place!" said the boy.

5. I saw my brother on television!

6. Did I like that movie? Yuck! No way!

Fluency Checkpoint *You have already listened to, practiced, and read the story. Read it again. Repeat until you can get all the words right and read it smoothly and with meaning.*

Read 📖 and repeat ↩.

Evaluation *Work with a partner to help each other evaluate your progress. Listen to each other read the story two times in row. When you are the reader, think about reading smoothly and with feeling. When you are the listener, pay attention to your partner's reading. Did it get smoother the second time? Did the reader use his or her voice to show the meaning of the words?*

_____

- -

I read the story two times to _____ .

I think that the second time I read was

My listener thinks that the second time I read was

Name _____ Date _____

Instant Words

Look 👁 and listen 👂.

find	pen
long	pencil
down	crayon
day	chalk
did	computer

Phrases *Read these phrases to yourself as you listen to them read aloud.*

Look 👁, listen 👂, and read 📖.

a good day	write on a board	crayon
find the answer	write with me	chalk
write down	find out things	computer
long and thin	pen	
write on paper	pencil	

Could you read every word? If not, repeat reading and listening until you can. Then, try reading the phrases on your own without listening.

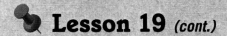

Name _____   Date _____

Game *This is not a story but a game. Follow along as you listen to it being read aloud. Do not try the game yet. First, repeat reading and listening until you know every word in the directions and in the game. Do that a few times to be sure you know all the words. You will play the game later.*

It is **a good day** to play a game. Will you play "What am I?"
Read each clue. **Find the answer** below. **Write down** the answer.

   pen   pencil   crayon   chalk   computer

1. I am **long and thin**. You **write on paper** with me. What am I?

2. I am white. You **write on a board** with me. What am I?

3. You **write with me,** too, but with ink. What am I?

4. I come in many colors. You can draw and color with me. What am I?

5. I have letters and numbers. You can **find out things** on me. What am I?

About the Game *Before you play the game, answer some questions about it. Follow along as each question is read. Then, answer the questions with words from the game.*

$$\boxed{\textbf{Look} \ \odot, \ \textbf{listen} \ , \ \textbf{and write} \ .}$$

                                                              _____
1.   What is the name of the game? - - - - - - - - - - - - - - -
                                                              _____

2.   What is one of the directions you are given?
   _____
   -
   _____ .

Name _____ Date _____

On Your Own *It is time to read and play the game. Write your answers on the lines.*

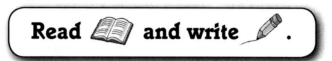

Read 📖 and write ✏️ .

It is a good day to play a game. Will you play "What am I?"
Read each clue. Find the answer below. Write the answer.

pen	pencil	crayon	chalk	computer

1. I am long and thin. You write on paper with me.

    What am I? -

    _____

2. I am white. You write on a board with me.

    What am I? -

    _____

3. You write with me, too, but with ink.

    What am I? -

    _____

4. I come in many colors. You can draw and color with me.

    What am I? -

    _____

5. I have letters and numbers. You can find out things on me.

    What am I? -

    _____

Learning About Reading: *Proofreading*

Listen 👂

There are only two kinds of sentences used in the game—telling sentences and asking sentences. Remember that telling sentences end with a period. Asking sentences end with a question mark. And, of course, all sentences begin with a capital letter! Get ready to see if you can find some mistakes in sentences.

Name _____ Date _____

Try It! *Uh-oh. These sentences are missing something at the end—a period or a question mark. If it is a telling sentence, add a period at the end. If it is an asking sentence, add a question mark at the end.*

Read and write .

1. I am long and thin

2. You write with me on paper

3. Am I a crayon

Fluency Checkpoint *You have already listened to, practiced, and read the story. Read it again. Repeat until you can get all the words right and read it smoothly and with meaning.*

Read and repeat .

Evaluation *Games are fun, but sometimes you have to figure out some new words to be able to play them. How do you think you are doing with figuring out new words? Listen as each statement is read. Circle the answer that sounds most like you.*

Circle That's me! or Not me!

I am learning to figure out new words by myself.   That's me!   Not me!

I get sometimes get stuck on words I haven't

seen before.   That's me!   Not me!

New words confuse me. I can't figure them

out on my own.   That's me!   Not me!

Name _____ Date _____

Special Lesson: Reader's Theater
Instant Words

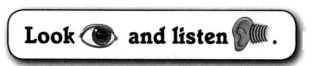

Look 👁 and listen 👂.

get   book

come   newspaper

made   magazine

may   sign

part   letter

Phrases *Read these phrases to yourself as you listen to them being read aloud.*

Look 👁, listen 👂, and read 📖.

where would we get	How would we get	the letter
let's get	do their part	may come by
newspapers, books, and magazines	send a letter	make a sign
they may have	come to get	may be on to something
have made money		

Could you read every word? If not, repeat reading and listening until you can. Then, try reading the phrases on your own without listening.

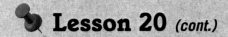

Name _____ Date _____

Story *Read the story to yourself as you listen to it read aloud. Repeat reading and listening until you know every word.*

Look 👁, listen 👂, and read 📖.

Tammy's school needed to raise money to buy new computers. Tammy's teacher, Mr. Shay, asked the class for ideas.

Jena:	We could have a plant sale.
Mr. Shay:	Yes, but **where would we get** plants to sell?
Tyler:	What if we had a pet show? We could bring our pets.
Mr. Shay:	Yes, but how would we make money?
Tammy:	I know! **Let's get** people to give us old **newspapers, books, and magazines they may have.** Lots of people **have made money** from recycling. We could, too!
Mr. Shay:	**How would we get** people to **do their part?**
Tammy:	We **send a letter** telling them that we will **come to get** their recyclables. They can start by recycling **the letter!**
Tyler:	It could also say that they **may come by** and drop them off.
Tammy:	We could **make a sign,** too.
Mr. Shay:	I think you **may be on to something,** Tammy. Let's go for it!

About the Story *Follow along and listen to each question. We will talk about our answers in a class discussion.*

Look 👁, listen 👂, and share.

1. What is the reason for the first part of the story?
2. In what special way is the rest of the story written?
3. Do you think collecting recyclables is a good idea for raising money?
4. If you were in the class, what idea for raising money would you offer?

Name _____ Date _____

On Your Own

Read 📖 and draw ✏️ .

We could have a plant sale.	We could have a pet show.
We could get newspapers, books, and magazines for recycling.	We made a sign about dropping off recyclables.

Learning About Reading: *Reader's Theater*

Listen  .

*Now it is time to put everything you have learned about reading into a fun idea called **reader's theater**. If the word* theater *makes you think of putting on a play or a performance, you are right. Reader's theater is kind of performance. Like a play, there are characters with parts to say. But, unlike a play, in reader's theater you don't memorize your lines. All you do is read your part from the script. You don't have to remember anything by heart, but you do have to be able to read your part and know when it is your turn.*

Besides the characters, there is one more part that is sometimes needed to perform reader's theater. That is someone who reads anything that is not said by one of the characters. This reader is called the narrator. In this story the narrator's words appear in slanted writing. The narrator introduces the story for the listeners.

Lesson 20 *(cont.)*

Name _____ Date _____

Try It! *You will be presenting the story as reader's theater. There are reading parts for five people. They are listed below. When you are given your part, fill in the sentence below.*

Read and write.

The five reading parts are Jena, Mr. Shay, Tyler, Tammy, and Narrator.

_____

I will be reading the part of _____ .

Fluency Checkpoint *You have already listened to, practiced, and read the story. Now practice it for a reader's theater presentation. You will work in a group of five students. You will have your part to read. Read and reread your part until you know it very well. Then, practice with your group, reading the story aloud until you all can do it smoothly together.*

Evaluation *How did you feel about doing reader's theater? Circle the number of stars that shows best what you think.*

How I prepared ★★★ ★★ ★   How my group prepared ★★★ ★★ ★

Working in a group ★★★ ★★ ★   Practicing together ★★★ ★★ ★

Following the parts ★★★ ★★ ★   Getting all the words right ★★★ ★★ ★

Performing ★★★ ★★ ★   Doing Reader's Theater ★★★ ★★ ★

92   #50288—Increasing Fluency with High Frequency Word Phrases Grade 1   © Shell Education

Lesson 1
▶ **About the Story** (page 14)
1. a little girl
2. a boy
3. of the boy
4. of the girl

▶ **On Your Own** (page 15)
Phrases illustrated appropriately.

▶ **Try It!** (page 16)
Underlined: girl, boy, man, woman, boy, girl, baby, girl

Lesson 2
▶ **About the Story** (page 18)
1. toy
2. it
3. in
4. that

▶ **On Your Own** (page 19)
Phrases illustrated appropriately.

▶ **Try It!** (page 20)
1. It is a doll.
2. Is it a game?
3. It is a train.
4. Is it a toy?

▶ **Evaluation**
doll

Lesson 3
▶ **About the Story** (page 22)
1. game
2. five
3. four

▶ **On Your Own** (page 23)
Phrases illustrated appropriately.

▶ **Try It!** (page 24)
1. to
2. for
3. in or on

Lesson 4
▶ **About the Story** (page 26)
1. pants and a shirt
2. a dress
3. a hat
4. one of his shoes
5. on the train

▶ **On Your Own** (page 27)
Phrases illustrated appropriately.

▶ **Try It!** (page 28)
1. two
2. two
3. three
4. four

▶ **Evaluation**
They dress the baby/in a shirt and shoes.

Lesson 5
▶ **About the Story** (page 30)
1. dog, fish
2. from
3. have

▶ **On Your Own** (page 31)
Phrases illustrated appropriately.

▶ **Try It!** (page 32)
this: dress, pants
at: hat, that, rabbit
be: three
have: of, five
from: game

Lesson 6
▶ **About the Story** (page 34)
1. at the desk
2. on the sofa
3. under the table

▶ **On Your Own** (page 35)
Phrases illustrated appropriately.

▶ **Try It!** (page 36)
1. baby
2. boy
3. under

Lesson 7
▶ **About the Story** (page 38)
1. nuts and birds
2. the birds
3. one nut

▶ **On Your Own** (page 39)
Phrases illustrated appropriately.

Answer Key (cont.)

▶ **Try It!** (page 40)
1. cup: up, pup
2. plate: ate, gate
3. nut: but, cut
4. words: birds

Lesson 8
▶ **About the Poem** (page 42)
1. said
2. your
▶ **On Your Own** (page 43)
Phrases illustrated appropriately.
▶ **Try It!** (page 44)
Will, drive, take, car
we, go, on, bus
try, luck, in, truck

Lesson 9
▶ **About the Story** (page 46)
1. Good for You
2. each
3. meat and bread
▶ **On Your Own** (page 47)
Words written and illustrated.
▶ **Try It!** (page 48)
Have an apple or some nuts.
Use your head to pick foods.
Make a sandwich with some bread and meat.
Each of these is good for you.
▶ **Evaluation** (page 48)
#2

Lesson 10
▶ **About the Story** (page 50)
1. her doll
2. Do you
3. their, their
▶ **On Your Own** (page 51)
Phrases illustrated appropriately.
▶ **Try It!** (page 52)
1. their
2. there
3. There
4. their

Lesson 11
▶ **About the Story** (page 54)
1. my birthday
2. seven
3. out in the yard
4. about eight o'clock
▶ **On Your Own** (page 55)
1. phrase
2. sentence
3. phrase
4. phrase
5. sentence
6. phrase
7. phrase
8. sentence
▶ **Try It!** (page 56)
1. I
2. S
3. T
▶ **Evaluation**
Sentences will vary.

Lesson 12
▶ **About the Story** (page 58)
1. pears, oranges, (bananas)
2. grapes
3. every day
▶ **On Your Own** (page 59)
Phrases illustrated appropriately.
▶ **Try It!** (page 60)
1. bowl (down)
2. fruit (up)
3. grapes (down)
4. juice (up)
5. fruit (up)
6. cereal (down)

Lesson 13
▶ **About the Story** (page 62)
1. in her chair
2. only grass
3. bushes, flowers, and trees
4. happy
▶ **On Your Own** (page 63)
Phrases illustrated appropriately.

Try It! (page 64)
1. garden. bushes.
2. trees. flowers.
3. birds. happy.
4. garden. garden.

Lesson 14
▶ **About the Story** (page 66)
1. a teacher
2. water
3. the sun
▶ **On Your Own** (page 67)
Phrases illustrated appropriately.
▶ **Try It!** (page 68)
1. rainy
2. likes
3. doing
4. looked
▶ **Evaluation**
Sentences will vary.

Lesson 15
▶ **About the Directions** (page 70)
1. a small lake
2. the sun and a cloud
3. four
4. small
▶ **On Your Own** (page 71)
Map drawn according to
the directions.
▶ **Try It!** (page 72)
1. no
2. yes
3. no
4. no
5. yes

Lesson 16
▶ **About the Story** (page 74)
Sentences will vary.
▶ **On Your Own** (page 75)
Scene drawn according to the directions.
▶ **Try It!** (page 76)
1. lake = long
2. farms = fields
3. will = hill

Lesson 17
▶ **About the Story** (page 78)
Student answers will vary.
▶ **On Your Own** (page 79)
Phrases illustrated appropriately.
▶ **Try It!** (page 80)
I had some cereal, and then some juice.
The juice was colder than the milk.

Lesson 18
▶ **About the Story** (page 82)
1. my big brother
2. at ball games
3. Saturday
▶ **On Your Own** (page 83)
Story parts drawn in order.

Lesson 19
▶ **About the Game** (page 86)
1. What am I?
2. Read each clue, find the answer below, or write down the answer.
▶ **On Your Own** (page 87)
1. pencil
2. chalk
3. pen
4. crayon
5. computer
▶ **Try It!** (page 88)
1. I am long and thin.
2. You write with me on paper.
3. Am I a crayon?

Lesson 20
▶ **About the Story** (page 90)
Students answer questions in a class discussion.
▶ **On Your Own** (page 91)
Phrases illustrated appropriately.
▶ **Try It!** (page 92)
Students participate in a reader's theater presentation.

References

Carroll, J. B. et.al. 1971. *Word frequency book*. New York: American Heritage.

Crystal, D. 1995. *The Cambridge encyclopedia of the English language*. Cambridge,UK: Cambridge University Press.

Fry, E. B., and J. E. Kress. 2006. *The reading teacher's book of lists*. 5th ed. San Francisco: Jossey-Bass.

Fry, E. B. 2000. 1000 *Instant words: The most common words for teaching reading, writing, and spelling*. Westminster, CA: Teacher Created Materials.

Fry, E. B. 1957. Developing a word list for remedial reading. *Elementary English* (November issue).

Report of the National Reading Panel. 2000. Washington DC: National Institute of Child Health and Human Development Clearinghouse.

Rasinski, T. V. 2003. *The fluent reader*. New York: Scholastic.

Rasinski, T. V., and N. D. Padak. 1998. How elementary students referred for compensatory reading instruction perform on school-based measures of word recognition, fluency, and comprehension. *Reading Psychology* 19:85–216.

Sakiey, E. H. 1977. Syllables: A weighted graphemic inventory. PhD diss., Rutgers University.

Samuels, S. J. 1979. The method of repeated readings. *The Reading Teacher* 32:403–408.

Samuels, S. J. 2002. Reading fluency: Its development and assessment. In *What research has to say about reading instruction*. 3rd ed. Ed. A. E. Farstrup and S. J. Samuels. Newark, DE: International Reading Association.